God's Approval on Your Ministry
A Practical Guide to Biblical Fasting

I would like to dedicate this book to my LORD and Saviour Jesus Christ. It is my prayer that He will use it for His glory and the salvation of many souls!

Table of Contents

"The work of a good book is to incite the reader to moral action, turn his eyes toward God and urge him forward. Beyond that it cannot go."

A.W. TOZER

Preface

Have you ever wondered what gets God's attention? As human beings and as Christians, we should want to know what gets the ear of an almighty God. Throughout the pages of the Word of God, stories are recorded of how the Almighty gave His attention to sinful human beings like you and me. Many stories and testimonies have a common Biblical thread—fasting.

Fasting is one of the most often overlooked and understudied topics in the Bible, yet it is one of the most important if we want God's attention. When we fast, we come before God with a sense of seriousness and soberness. I believe that when we fast we prove to ourselves and to God just how important a prayer request is to us.

Throughout my years as a pastor, I have seen the results and benefits of fasting in my life and the lives of others. I have seen God assist me in personal health needs because of a fast. I have seen God move obstacles and hindrances to my ministry because of a fast. There have been times in my ministry when I drove myself to fast because of a desire for God to work, and there have been times when God has driven me to fast because of His desire to work. No matter what the situation is, fasting plays a deep and vital role in our spiritual and physical lives as Christians.

The author, Dr. Mike Van Horn, is a man that I can honestly say has seen the blessings of fasting. In *God's Approval on Your Ministry*, he takes the time to give the Biblical reasoning behind fasting and the necessity of it for God to place His stamp of approval on your ministry. I have seen God open doors for this man that I believe would never have opened without his fasting before the LORD.

There has never been a more urgent time for God to work in our lives and ministries than now. As Christians, we need God to place His hand on our lives, and we need Him to do the work that we could never do. We need God's attention and His approval, but are we willing to go without to receive it?

Dr. Mike Norris, Pastor
Franklin Road Baptist Church

One of the missing elements in Christianity today is the fundamental teaching on fasting. As Christians, there are certain duties and responsibilities we can perform based on our experience and knowledge of Scripture. However, there are undeniable circumstances and challenges we face in the ministry that can only be overcome by fasting and prayer. Jesus said, "This kind can come forth by nothing, but by prayer and fasting" *(Mark 9:29)*. Dr. Van Horn provides an excellent work in this book, rightly dividing the Scripture on the Biblical teaching of fasting. Herein lies the secret to receiving great power, overcoming difficult circumstances, and receiving the necessary resources for our work.

Dr. Terry R. Ellis, President
Rock of Ages Ministries

"As Christians, we need God to place His hand on our lives, and we need Him to do the work that we could never do. We need God's attention and His approval, but are we willing to go without to receive it?"

DR. MIKE NORRIS

Introduction

Hidden inside the pages of God's marvelous Word are secrets that will anoint our ministries and unleash the powers from Heaven to accomplish the task He has given us. Dr. Ron Gearis said Psalm 119:18 was one of his favorite verses: "Open thou mine eyes, that I may behold wondrous things out of thy law." He went on to say, "It might be one of my most used verses. I am sure I don't use it as much as God would like for me to use [it]...."[1] I am certain that most Christians in the world do not think to ask God to open their eyes to His Word. Let us ask the LORD to open our eyes during this study to see the wondrous things He has in store for us.

God has given us a wonderful Book that has been preserved for us through the ages. "For ever, O LORD, thy word is settled in heaven" *(Psalm 119:89)*. It is loaded with promises and avails us of limitless power, with which to accomplish many great things for our Saviour during our lifetime. It must be opened, read, studied, meditated upon, and applied if we hope to receive all the benefits God has in store for us.

> This book of the law shall not depart out of thy mouth; but thou shalt meditate therein day and night, that thou mayest observe to do according to all that is written therein: for then thou shalt make thy way prosperous, and then thou shalt have good success. *(Joshua 1:8)*

This verse should be the rule used when seeking God's approval. When you memorize, meditate, and agree to do what this verse says, success is guaranteed! God is a promise keeper. If it is your desire to be a prosperous and successful Christian, then the guidelines presented in the pages to follow are vital.

God has given us many signs of the preservation of His Word through the ages, but in modern times, one sign comes to my attention. As far as I know, this miracle was never reported on CNN or any other conservative or liberal news media. September 11, 2001, was a day that will be remembered by most Americans as a day of great destruction by terrorist attacks. Our country had not been violated in this fashion since the Japanese attacked Pearl Harbor on December 7, 1941. The Twin Towers were destroyed, the Pentagon was severely damaged, and a horrific crash happened in a field just outside the small village of Shanksville, Pennsylvania, because a group of true Americans on Flight 93 fought the terrorists and kept them from doing further damage. Journalist Tom Lavis of the *Tribune Democrat* wrote an article entitled "Symbol of Faith," which, if widely publicized, would and should cause the world to take a look at the Bible in a different light.

Bible Survives Fiery Flight 93 Crash

If the world is looking for a sign of hope in the turmoil that erupted on September 11, 2001, it may have found it. Teams of emergency personnel who responded to the crash of Flight 93 near Shanksville made an amazing discovery that shocked and inspired them. Resting not far from the smoldering, 25-foot-deep crater where 40 innocent victims perished, firefighters found a Bible that was barely singed.[2]

This remarkable article reveals to us that God has preserved His Word for us in this contemporary world so we can know His mind. "For who hath known the mind of the LORD, that he may instruct him? But we have the mind of Christ" *(1 Corinthians 2:16)*. Critics have discredited it, the devil questioned it, haters of God have tried to burn it, educators ridicule it, and our federal government has tried to remove it from all government institutions, but God has preserved it forever! It could be that God just wanted to show the world that even a literal fire that consumed everything in just minutes could not burn what He has established as truth!

It is interesting to note that the presence of the Bible found at the crash scene in Shanksville gave comfort to many, unlike the deadly day of the massacre in Jonestown, Guyana, where no Bibles were found on the compound:

As the army troops (the grave registration unit) withdrew from Guyana, some new evidence came to light, which was almost passed over. The Major in charge of the army operation reported with utter amazement, 'There were no Bibles in Jonestown!' [3]

According to another article on the web, coroners found another Bible in a warehouse where articles that belonged to the victims were stored. "Local coroner Wallace Miller will later come across a second Bible at the warehouse where the Flight 93 victims' belongings are kept."[4]

There were God-fearing men and women aboard Flight 93 that day, men and women who knew how to pray and, if truth be known, who may have even experienced answered prayer through fasting.

One of those men was Todd Beamer. We often hear the last words he spoke before overtaking the terrorists, "Let's roll," but we seldom hear what he said to the 911 operator prior to that heroic phrase. These were the words this brave American said while thousands of feet above the ground, moments before he would crash to his death: "Our Father which art in heaven, Hallowed be thy name."[5] He knew that he was going to see his Saviour face to face very soon, and God gave him the courage to do what he had to do. The Bible was the source that gave these heroic men their strength. The call of God on one's life is by far the highest calling of all. In his book, *Heartbeats of the Holy*, Keith E. Knauss made this statement, "Great is the burden of that holy calling and great are the consequences of neglecting it. It is an unceasing Gethsemane that besets the heart and mind and soul of one so privileged to stand before men in the stead of God."[6] Wow! What an honor it is to be the spokesman for the magnificent God of Heaven! Brother Knauss went on to say,

> It is doubtful if God regards any calling on earth as higher or more sacred than that of the ministry. Henry Ward Beecher said, in a lecture to students at Yale, "God stands at the door of the womb of nature and calls men to birth. When a quarter of a man is born he says, 'Stand aside!' When a half man is born He again says, 'Stand aside!' When three quarters of a man is born He still says, 'Stand aside!' But when a whole man is born God says, 'Come forth; here is my preacher!' [7]

It is, or should be, the desire of every Christian and every preacher to have God smile on their lives and ministries. Just like a child's heart jumps with joy to see his parents smiling at him during a school play, a Christian should have the aspiration to have the Heavenly Father's approval of his accomplishments.

There are many ingredients required in order to have God's approval on your ministry. We will explore many of them in the pages to follow. One of these elements is fasting. The main content of this book is to help you see the importance of fasting for spiritual and health reasons. When we review Christian history, we see that the great heroes of the faith all practiced fasting in some form. Fasting seems to be the seldom used avenue to reach the ears of God. The pages of this book are planned to introduce you to or to rekindle in you this wonderful way to access the Throne Room of God with your needs.

In this evil day when all the forces of Hell are against the church, we must implement all weaponry God has in His arsenal for our use. The devil is out to destroy our marriages, children, ministries, and our personal relationship with God. God has and always will use prayer, fasting, righteous living, and the Bible to combat the devil and the forces of Hell: "For I am the LORD, I change not; therefore ye sons of Jacob are not consumed" *(Malachi 3:6)*.

Whenever a new weapon is introduced to the armed forces, it goes through many stringent tests to evaluate its ability to accomplish the task for which it was designed. Prayer, fasting, righteous living, and the Bible have been tried and tested throughout the ages of Christianity and have effectively kept the Christian on top of his game. If we want our ministry to be one that God approves to be part of His holy weaponry, it must be developed through the guidelines He has recorded for us in His "Training Manual." Fasting is a very powerful weapon that God has appointed to break down the strongholds the Devil places in our way. "For the weapons of our warfare are not carnal, but mighty through God to the pulling down of strong holds;" *(2 Corinthians 10:4)*.

Fasting is one of the seldom used avenues to reach the heart of God. Fasting coupled with prayer can and will unleash God's hand in your ministry, desires, and needs. When Queen Esther accepted her call to go before the king to intercede on behalf of the Israelites, she told Mordecai to gather the people together and begin fasting. She did not tell him to have them pray (no doubt they were praying), but she told them to add fasting to their prayers. The rest is history!

In his book *Shaping History through Prayer and Fasting*, Derek Prince makes this statement: "Without a doubt, the Devil is behind this theory that Christians must only fast in secret. It deprives God's people of the most powerful weapon in their whole armory—that of united, public fasting." [8]

Many are not able to tap into the magnificent power available to Christians simply because of a lack of knowledge. The prophet Hosea told us of the dangers of lack of knowledge.

> My people are destroyed for lack of knowledge: because thou hast rejected knowledge, I will also reject thee, that thou shalt be no priest to me: seeing thou hast forgotten the law of thy God, I will also forget thy children. *(Hosea 4:6)*

In essence, we have limited God from using His full force in our lives. "Yea, they turned back and tempted God, and limited the Holy One of Israel" *(Psalms 78:41)*. The only time the word *limited* is used in the King James Bible is found in this verse regarding God's people hindering Him from pouring out the blessings!

There is very little doubt that the average Christian is not using all the resources God has made available to His children to have a victorious Christian life in this present generation. In the book *Shaping History Through Prayer and Fasting*, Derek Prince makes this statement:

> The alternatives that confront us are clearly presented by Paul in Romans: 'Be not overcome of evil, but overcome evil with good' *(Romans 12:21)*. There are only two choices: either to overcome or to be overcome. There is no middle way, no third course open to us.[9]

There must be a great urgency for us to fortify our Christian lives so we can stand between Hell and sinners to introduce them to our Saviour with the power of God!

Throughout the Bible, we will see many different reasons for fasting, coupled with different types and ways to conduct your fast, all leaving you with instruction on how to receive answers to your prayer. For example, Christ fasted from Heaven. Our Saviour denied Himself of many pleasures as well as essentials for living. The Creator of the universe and heir of all things had no place to lay his dear head. He could have stayed in Heaven but chose to fast from the very presence of the Father for thirty-three and one-half years so you and I could enjoy forgiveness and spend eternity in Heaven! He also started His earthly ministry with a forty-day water-only fast.

> (15) For we have not an high priest which cannot be touched with the feeling of our infirmities; but was in all points tempted like as we are, yet without sin. (16) Let us therefore come boldly unto the throne of grace, that we may obtain mercy, and find grace to help in time of need. *(Hebrews 4:15, 16)*

All this He endured, to help us understand that through His power we, too, can achieve great and mighty things for God by approaching His Throne through prayer and fasting.

From Heaven's perspective, God fasted from His Son. God the Father watched from Glory as His dear Son suffered and died for all mankind. It was when Christ was on the cross that God turned His back on Him, fasting from His Son so redemption's plan could unfold. Oh, what love salvation's plan displays!

We will learn the reasons for fasting, types of fasts, length of fasts, results from fasting, and the power through fasting in the pages to follow.

This study will include many testimonies of victories through fasting from modern-day preachers and laymen. We have great testimonies of preachers of old practicing fasting, but it is necessary to hear the testimonies of God's unlimited power through the avenue He still honors—fasting. We need to know that our contemporary preachers are still tapping into God's limitless power to accomplish His will for ministry and personal victories.

> (1) We have heard with our ears, O God, our fathers have told us, what work thou didst in their days, in the times of old. (2) How thou didst drive out the heathen with thy hand, and plantedst them; how thou didst afflict the people, and cast them out. (3) For they got not the land in possession by their own sword, neither did their own arm save them: but thy right hand, and thine arm, and the light of thy countenance, because thou hadst a favour unto them. *(Psalm 44:1-3)*

The next generation of Christians is counting on us to deliver the same spiritual achievements that D.L. Moody, R.A. Torrey, David Livingston, John R. Rice, Oswald Chambers, Charles Spurgeon, C.T. Studd, and other great men of old passed on for our learning. If we do not show them that the same God who made the ministries of these great heroes of the faith productive and powerful can and will make ours great, too, we could hinder them from achieving all that God wants from them.

Nothing you will read in this study is, in any way, to be considered medical advice. I highly recommend that you seek the counsel of your physician before you practice fasting for long periods of time.

It is of the utmost importance that the spiritual leaders of today make themselves known to this power source God has given us.

CHAPTER ONE

GOD'S APPROVAL
On Your Ministry

(1) We then, as workers together with him, beseech you also that ye receive not the grace of God in vain. (2) (For he saith, I have heard thee in a time accepted, and in the day of salvation have I succoured thee: behold, now is the accepted time; behold, now is the day of salvation.) (3) Giving no offence in any thing, that the ministry be not blamed: (4) But in all things approving ourselves as the ministers of God, in much patience, in afflictions, in necessities, in distresses, (5) In stripes, in imprisonments, in tumults, in labours, in watchings, in fastings; *(2 Corinthians 6:1-5)*

You will have many co-workers in a lifetime; some carry their own weight, while others depend on everyone else. Christians are privileged to work together with "HIM" in our ministries and our every-day lives. We must remember that God has not dumped us off in a world of sinners expecting us to live a victorious Christian life or to carry the load of a ministry by ourselves. He is actively working together with us to see that we are successful, productive, and blessed in our way. Oswald Chambers said:

> The Holy Spirit always works through human instrumentality, and there is never any possibility of pride when the Holy Spirit uses us. We are empowered into union with Christ by the Holy Ghost. [10]

With this thought in mind, when we fast, we will not be alone either; Christ will sustain us in our time of need.

Born-again, Bible-believing Christians are the only people of faith who actually have the God of Heaven dwelling in them. "But if the Spirit of him that raised up Jesus from the dead dwell in you, he that raised up Christ from the dead shall also quicken your mortal bodies by his Spirit that dwelleth in you" *(Romans 8:11)*. The blessed Holy Ghost lives inside of believers guiding us in all truth! Many other religions practice fasting in vain only to hope they find approval from their god. Works-oriented religions often include self-inflicted practices to show their gods their loyalty with false hopes of an eternity in paradise. The false prophets of Baal are a good example of this activity: "And they cried aloud, and cut themselves after their manner with knives and lancets, till the blood gushed out upon them" *(1 Kings 18:28).*

In the book *Heartbeat of the Holy*, Keith E. Knauss made this plea for the touch of the Spirit:

> Oh of the touch and wisdom of the Spirit of God. It is He who will give our hands the touch of a surgeon to rightly divide the Word. It is He who will grant us wisdom to use the sacred balances in weighing out the proper portions of manna for the needs of our people. It is He who will season our speech with the grace that His Word be made more beautiful and our LORD more glorified. It is He who will press the live coal from the altar to our lips and open our mouths that we may show forth the praises of the LORD, or else we shall not speak with power. [11]

The indwelling of the blessed Holy Ghost is the secret weapon that believers have to accomplish great things for God while living in this present evil world. It is He that will guide you into your fast, and it is He that will sustain you during your fast. Derek Prince penned these words:

> In the world is the spirit of antichrist, working toward the emergence of Antichrist himself. In the disciples of Christ is the Holy Spirit, holding back the emergence of Antichrist. Thus, the disciples who are indwelled by the Holy Spirit act as a barrier, holding back the climax of lawlessness and the final emergence of Antichrist. [12]

The indwelling of the blessed Holy Ghost is the strength from which we draw. It is He that gives us the power to endure the trials caused by fasting and gives us the boldness to stand before the forces of Hell to conclude the time set apart to fast.

Oswald Chambers said, "The servant of God has to go through the experience of things before he is allowed to go through the study of them." [13] In essence, he is saying that in order to teach it, you must have lived it. Men who have experienced God's marvelous works through fasting must teach fasting to the future generation of Christians.

It is of the utmost importance that the spiritual leaders of today make themselves known to this power source God has given us. Fasting can release the bonds of sin from the addicted individual, it can produce great spiritual awakenings in the heart of the Christian leader and his followers, and it will be recognized and rewarded by our LORD. How sad it is that most Christians are deprived of this great power source!

Please understand that your fast will in no way back God into a corner, forcing Him to answer your prayer the way you desire. On the contrary, your fast will allow the LORD the liberty to answer the way He chooses!

If we are going to see great results in our ministries, we must associate ourselves with the list of trials the apostle Paul endured during his ministry on earth and the elements of tapping into God's power that he implemented.

Paul lists the elements for the approval of our ministry coupled with the importance of our ministry being found blameless. First he says, "...in much patience..." (2 Corinthians 6:4). A ministry that will be blameless demands endurance in all areas. Noah Webster gives four definitions for the word patient: [14]

1. Having the quality of enduring evils without murmuring or fretfulness; sustaining afflictions of body or mind with fortitude, calmness or Christian submission to the divine will; as a patient person, or a person of patient temper.

2. Not easily provoked; calm under the sufferance of injuries or offenses; not revengeful. Be patient towards all men. 1 Thessalonians 5:14.

3. Persevering; constant in pursuit or exertion; calmly diligent. Whatever I have done is due to patient thought.

4. Not hasty; not over eager or impetuous; waiting or expecting with calmness or without discontent. Not patient to expect the turns of fate.

Someone once said that the ministry would be wonderful if it were not for people. I am sure it was said in jest, but the truth is, without people we have no ministry. No doubt "patience" was mentioned first in Paul's list, for without it no man could endure the rest of the list: afflictions, necessities, distresses, stripes, imprisonments, tumults, labours, watchings, and fastings. Each of these elements, with the exception of watchings and fastings, are inflicted by or included among other people. He then listed the ingredients that will produce the patience needed to overcome each of these trials. Keith Knauss said,

> Our LORD did not call soft-palmed, lily-fingered sons of pleasure to herald His saving message. He went down to the sea and called some brawny-muscled, horny-handed fisherman, used to pulling oars in the teeth of the fierce storms of Gennersaret. God called real men.[15]

The ministry is not for sissies, nor is the successful Christian life! It is a life of faith, stamina, labor, and heartaches; in all of which we must have the help of the LORD. Fasting will demand patience as well; you may receive an answer for your prayer right away, or God may say, "Wait."

When studying the Bible, we see that the Apostle Paul went through each one of these hardships and many more *(2 Corinthians 11:23-28)*; this leads me to conclude that we, too, must endure many hardships for a ministry that God approves. We must also conclude, through the inspired Word of God, that we can learn how to tap into the same power source the Apostle Paul and others used to do great things for God! Paul fasted at the beginning of his ministry while seeking God's direction and His approval.

Now that we have seen the list of elements involved in the ministry, let us continue to see how to obtain the power needed to have a ministry that has God's stamp of approval on it.

> (6) By pureness, by knowledge, by longsuffering, by kindness, by the Holy Ghost, by love unfeigned, (7) By the word of truth, by the power of God, by the armour of righteousness on the right hand and on the left, (8) By honour and dishonour, by evil report and good report: as deceivers, and yet true; (9) As unknown, and yet well known; as dying, and, behold, we live; as chastened, and not killed; (10) As sorrowful, yet alway rejoicing; as poor, yet making many rich; as having nothing, and yet possessing all things. *(2 Corinthians 6:6-10)*

Pureness is the element first mentioned in acquiring the approval of your ministry. Fasting is a form of purification. It will purge your body of toxins and can purge your mind from poisons that can destroy you.

The command is given concerning our behavior as Christians: "… Be ye holy; for I am holy" *(1 Peter 1:16)*. Another word that could be used for pureness is *blameless*. We are to maintain personal holiness in our lives because we represent the very Person of holiness! The world is filled with people who do not attend church because they believe the church is filled with hypocrites. Pureness pins the badge of power on our lapels giving us authority to go in His power to accomplish His will. Without this pureness in our lives, we too, will be labeled as hypocrites.

One time I was on visitation in the open dorm area of an adult state prison in Mississippi. During these visitation times we go into the inmates' living quarters, soul win, visit with them, and encourage them to come to our evening services. I stopped to talk to an inmate who was on his bunk; concerned about his eternal destination, I first asked if he knew Christ. He informed me that he was a saved man. As we continued our conversation, I noticed a magazine on his footlocker. This magazine was in no way good for him, so I encouraged him not to fill his mind with pictures that cause him to sin. It was not a hard-core porn magazine, but the cover had a girl in a swimsuit that did not have enough material on it to cover a ladybug. This advice caused his defensive mode to kick in! He asked me if I had a family; I told him about my wife, son, and little girl. He then proceeded to ask me what my wife and daughter wore when they went to the pool. Good question! In my heart I thanked the LORD that we have standards in our home and informed him that we did not go to public swimming pools. I was not going to allow my family to dress in their undergarments and parade around in front of a bunch of people in theirs! This testimony caused him to soften his heart, and for the next ten or fifteen minutes, I was able to be a help and a blessing to this man.

God will grant you power because of the personal holiness you decide to implement in your personal life. We must be careful not to allow our personal holiness to cause us to become self-righteous. David gives God the credit for his righteousness: "Hear me when I call, O God of my righteousness: thou hast enlarged me when I was in distress; have mercy upon me, and hear my prayer" *(Psalm 4:1)*. It is essential that we give God all the glory for anything accomplished through fasting and prayer. If He is lifted up, He will draw men toward Him.

God holds a special place in His heart for those who choose to live holy: "But know that the LORD hath set apart him that is godly for himself: the LORD will hear when I call unto him" *(Psalm 4:3)*. This, if nothing else, should cause us to live a holy life. It is estimated that there were no less than ten thousand men in the city of Sodom.[16] God was willing to save an entire city if He could have found one in a thousand who loved Him and served Him. We see this same thought in Job's thinking when he said, (23) "If there be a messenger with him, an interpreter, one among a thousand, to shew unto man his uprightness: (24) Then he is gracious unto him, and saith, Deliver him from going down to the pit: I have found a ransom" *(Job 33:23, 24)*. It also comes to our attention from the words of the preacher: "Which yet my soul seeketh, but I find not: one man among a thousand have I found; but a woman among all those have I not found" *(Ecclesiastes 7:28)*. My how it must grieve the heart of our precious LORD that so few people are willing to seek a life of holiness! In essence holiness is fasting from the world! The entire city of Sodom could have found mercy if one in a thousand were righteous and had a life of prayer and fasting. Lot was too busy feasting and playing instead of fasting and praying. This cost him his wife, children, and reputation.

The Bible gives us detailed outlines about our personal holiness. The problem is most will not implement these standards for living. The statement has been said over and over again: "That is not my conviction!" How can God's clear instruction not be your conviction? The fact is that unconfessed sins produce powerless Christians.

We must deny ourselves of what the world calls normal if we want God's blessings on our lives. This is a form of fasting too. David was doing his best when he penned the inspired words: "(4) I have not sat with vain persons, neither will I go in with dissemblers. (5) I have hated the congregation of evil doers; and will not sit with the wicked" *(Psalm 26:4)*. He refrained or fasted from going places where he knew he would be tempted.

Inside the living rooms of most Americans is a television. It is unnecessary to expound on the contents of most networks viewed on what has been referred to as "the one-eyed demon," but imagine George Washington passing through the threshold of time and viewing the filth that is on the screen today. No doubt he would be totally appalled. Christians have desensitized their minds by allowing such wickedness to enter into their minds daily through the eye gate. Just like any tool, television can be used in a good way. There are many good programs, and, used wisely, it can be entertaining and instructional. The Bible gives us clear instruction about our eyes:

(2) I will behave myself wisely in a perfect way. O when wilt thou come unto me? I will walk within my house with a perfect heart. (3) I will set no wicked thing before mine eyes: I hate the work of them that turn aside; it shall not cleave to me. *(Psalm 101:2, 3)*

According to the United States Department of Labor, "Watching

TV was the leisure activity that occupied the most time (2.7 hours per day), accounting for about half of leisure time, on average, for those age 15 and over." [17]   Imagine what could be accomplished in the prayer closet if this time was exchanged for a season of fasting and prayer!

> (1) And I, brethren, when I came to you, came not with excellency of speech or of wisdom, declaring unto you the testimony of God. (2) For I determined not to know any thing among you, save Jesus Christ, and him crucified. (3) And I was with you in weakness, and in fear, and in much trembling. (4) And my speech and my preaching was not with enticing words of man's wisdom, but in demonstration of the Spirit and of power: *(1 Corinthians 2:1-4)*

Going back to 2 Corinthians 6, we see that knowledge is essential to show ourselves approved. We are told to "Study to shew thyself approved unto God, a workman that needeth not to be ashamed, rightly dividing the word of truth" *(2 Timothy 2:15)*. People know if you know! Just like a dog can sense fear, people know if you have knowledge of the topic you are discussing. It takes time and discipline to acquire knowledge. Having degrees on your wall does not mean that you are any more spiritual than someone else. It is a dangerous practice to compare yourself to other men. "For we dare not make ourselves of the number, or compare ourselves with some that commend themselves: but they measuring themselves by themselves, and comparing themselves among themselves, are not wise" *(2 Corinthians 10:12)*. However, having an earned degree does show that you are willing to discipline yourself to obtain a formal education that will be beneficial in your work and labor for the LORD.

In the changing world we live in, many facets of the ministry will require some form of higher learning. Whether it be teaching character in the public schools or doing the work of a chaplain in the prisons, many of these positions now require a formal degree.

Keith E. Knauss made this statement concerning the preacher and his education: "He who accepts the call to the ministry should understand that by that act he dedicates himself to a lifelong studentship, without a college vacation. Death alone can grant the graduating diploma." [18]   It has been said that a preacher who does not read will dry up really quickly. We must always try to learn more and more. Knauss went on to make this statement that is hard but true: "The Holy Spirit simply will not sanction mental indolence, and endorse the needless ignorance of a minister, who in this age of schools, books, and opportunities, is too lazy to study and learn."[19]

Next, we see the element of longsuffering. This is an attribute that describes the love God has for the lost and dying world: "But thou, O LORD, art a God full of compassion, and gracious, longsuffering, and plenteous in mercy and truth" *(Psalm 86:15)*. We, too, must show this attribute to those around us. Not every new convert will grow at the rate we would like him to, neither will co-workers always be what you expect them to be. This does not mean we should abandon them but continue to work with them.

Paul was quick to get rid of John Mark, but later saw his usefulness in the ministry and invited him back: "Only Luke is with me. Take Mark, and bring him with thee: for he is profitable to me for the ministry" *(2 Timothy 4:11)*.

Each man has a gift that will differ from others. The best way to have a productive ministry is to evaluate each man's gift and allow him to work inside this gift. A great team is composed of men with a diversity of gifts and liberty to use them:

> (10) He that descended is the same also that ascended up far above all heavens, that he might fill all things.) (11) And he gave some, apostles; and some, prophets; and some, evangelists; and some, pastors and teachers; (12) For the perfecting of the saints, for the work of the ministry, for the edifying of the body of Christ: *(Ephesians 4:10-12)*

Over the long haul, those who enter the ministry will have many opportunities to display longsuffering. Dealing with people and ministry situations demands longsuffering!

After longsuffering comes kindness. "And be ye kind one to another, tenderhearted, forgiving one another, even as God for Christ's sake hath forgiven you" *(Ephesians 4:32)*. We are commanded to be kind, even to those who may be in a lower status in our eyes, for in God's eyes we are all the same. He is no respecter of persons: "Then Peter opened his mouth, and said, Of a truth I perceive that God is no respecter of persons" *(Acts 10:34)*. We never know what the person we are dealing with is going through. When a Baptist preacher checks into a hotel and treats the lady behind the counter like a dog, he will lose any possibility of ministering to her needs. Kindness opens up the door to give Godly counsel to those in need. Pride is the dominating sin that leads men to be rude: "Only by pride cometh contention: but with the well advised is wisdom" *(Proverbs 13:10)*.

We are then reminded that the work is completed "...by the Holy Ghost, by love unfeigned" *(2 Corinthians 6:6)*. The word *unfeigned* means genuine, not counterfeit. We know that the word *Christian* means Christ-like. Christ is love, true love, one that produces action! He loved the world so much that He laid His life down so we could live! This kind of love, which is produced by the "...word of truth, by the power of God..." must be evident in our lives if we want a successful ministry. Who are we to love? If we are Christ-like, we will love those He loves!

The date was January 12, 1979; the place was Andale, Kansas, a small farming community just outside of Wichita, Kansas. A fifteen-year-old girl was on her way to a basketball game just two blocks away from her home. It was a cold night, and blizzard conditions had set in. She never made it to that game that evening. A man came up from behind her, put a knife to her throat, forced her to get into his car, and took her out into the country and brutally raped her. He then made her get out of the car, took his knife, stabbed her in the throat, and left her alongside of the road to die. God was very gracious to this young girl; she was able to keep her senses and did not panic. She noticed two houses close by; one was about a half a mile away, but the lights were not on. The other house was one mile away with the lights glowing. She concluded that she had a better chance of someone being home there. She began to run towards this house with her hand pressing tightly against her wound; she remembered this procedure from a first aid class. She thought about cutting through the field but decided that if she died in the field it would be months before her body would be found and did not want to put her family through that kind of trauma, so she continued down the road and the long lane to the house.

When she arrived at the front door, she began to bang on it hoping someone was home to help. Thank God there was! An elderly couple lived in the home, and their daughter, a registered nurse, was there for a visit. They immediately called 911, began to get her warmed, and kept pressure on the wound. Her ambulance ride was one she will always remember. Over and over she quoted a memorized prayer her religion had taught her. She knew that she was not bad enough to go to Hell and did not think she was good enough to go to Heaven; so, as per her religious training, she hoped her prayers would help her find favor with God.

She survived the trauma and continued on with her life. Four years later I met Paula Winter for the first time and fell in love with her. Her neck had the scars of her abuse, and naturally it came up in conversation while we were dating. I was not active in church at the time, but I was a born-again Christian, and I knew what God said about salvation. I asked her if she knew she would be in Heaven if she had died that night. She told me about her testimony of praying and hoping that she was good enough to be taken from purgatory and placed in Heaven someday. I did not know anything about her religion, but I knew that was not what the Bible says it takes to be saved. I then told her salvation's great plan, and she prayed that night to receive Jesus Christ as her personal LORD and Saviour! Glory to His holy name!

Twenty years after her abduction and rape, God called us to the Rock of Ages Prison Ministry. I was attending the first Faith Promise Missions Conference at my father's church, Calvary Baptist Church in Crestline, Ohio. Dad surrendered to preach when he was fifty-seven years old, studied for two years, and took this church for his first pastorate at age sixty. God showed me His will for my life in this meeting. Paula was at our home church at a baby shower that evening. When I went home that night, I told her that God had just sentenced me to life in prison! She had the choice between one of two things to say that night: she had every right to tell me that she was not going to spend the rest of her life being a part of telling murderers and rapists about God's love. What she told me was an amazing display of unfeigned love. She said, that night when God looked down, He saw two sinners lost and on their way to Hell, an innocent little girl stuck in a religion of no hope and a wicked sinner. "If God can save me, He can save them, too!" Paula has given her testimony at a number of ladies' meetings, and it has been used over and over to help ladies who have been abused. Her testimony can be heard in full on our website, *www.vanhornroa.com*.

To love someone who has hurt you is a demonstration of God's amazing love for the world of sinners! The words Christ used on the cross, "...Father, forgive them; for they know not what they do..." *(Luke 23:34)* gives us the perfect example of unfeigned love! When we exercise this love in our ministries and in our personal lives, God gives us the power to accomplish great and mighty things for Him! I thank the LORD for my darling wife and her willingness to understand that "...all things work together for good to them that love God, to them who are the called according to his purpose" *(Romans 8:28)*. Romans 8:29 gives us the results of allowing tragedy to become a triumph: "For whom he did foreknow, he also did predestinate to be conformed to the image of his Son, that he might be the firstborn among many brethren." Displaying His love to a world of sinners will produce many souls that will be born again into the family of God. If Christ was willing to give His life so the person who harmed us could be saved, who are we to wish them to Hell? Unfeigned love is unconditional and not counterfeit. People know if you care!

Personal righteousness in every area of our lives is one of the key elements to the approval of our ministry: "...by the armour of righteousness on the right hand and on the left" *(2 Corinthians 6:7)*. Hidden sins will be in the open someday: "But if ye will not do so, behold, ye have sinned against the LORD: and be sure your sin will find you out" *(Numbers 32:23)*.

Pride is one of the biggest enemies we will face. We must guard ourselves from ever taking full credit for the success of our ministry: "God hath spoken once; twice have I heard this; that power belongeth unto God" *(Psalm 62:11)*.

Some men feel as if they have reached a level of Christianity where they will never fall. Christ admonished His disciples while teaching them to pray by giving them instruction on specific areas of life that will demand frequent prayer. One of His requests that should continually come off of our lips is to ask God to keep us from temptation and to deliver us from evil. We must allow God to get involved in keeping us clean!

In Psalm 26, we see David on top of his game; he seems to be in a great relationship with the LORD. In verses 1 and 2, he is asking God to make a close examination of his heart and mind: "(1) Judge me, O LORD; for I have walked in mine integrity: I have trusted also in the LORD; therefore I shall not slide. (2) Examine me, O LORD, and prove me; try my reins and my heart." In verse 3, he tells of his love for God's Word and walking in the truth: "For thy lovingkindness is before mine eyes: and I have walked in thy truth." Christ also says, "Sanctify them through thy truth: thy word is truth" *(John 17:17)*. In verses 4 and 5, he tells how he has refrained from fellowshipping with evil men: "(4) I have not sat with vain persons, neither will I go in with dissemblers. (5) I have hated the congregation of evil doers; and will not sit with the wicked." Then we see in verse 6 his desire to pray and confess his weakness and sin to God: "I will wash mine hands in innocency: so will I compass thine altar, O LORD." Verse 7 describes his desire to be a soul winner: "That I may publish with the voice of thanksgiving, and tell of all thy wondrous works." Verse 8 gives a clear description of his love for the house of God: "LORD, I have loved the habitation of thy house, and the place where thine honour dwelleth." After this list of elements that gives him the joy and power to be a dedicated man of God, we see his prayer for God's help to keep him from sin in verses 9 and 10: "(9) Gather not my soul with sinners, nor my life with bloody men: (10) In whose hands is mischief, and their right hand is full of bribes." In the last two verses of the chapter, we see David making the proclamation that it was his choice to serve God with all of his heart: "(11) But as for me, I will walk in mine integrity: redeem me, and be merciful unto me. (12) My foot standeth in an even place: in the congregations will I bless the LORD."

David truly was on top of his game and had a great walk with God at this time. Something drastic must have taken place between Psalm 26 and Psalm 51. In chapter 51, David is crying out to God for mercy and forgiveness because of his dreadful sin with Bathsheba. Somewhere along the line he became self-confident in his own righteousness and forgot to ask God for His help to keep him from temptation and deliver him from evil! We must always realize that if there be any good in us, it comes from God above, and it will be by His help that we do not become a castaway!

"By honour and dishonour, by evil report and good report: as deceivers, and yet true" *(2 Corinthians 6:8)*. We will have people who will love us and those who will detest us as we labor for Him; sometimes it will be our closest friends who will abandon us. King David experienced this with his dear friend Ahithophel:

> (12) For it was not an enemy that reproached me; then I could have borne it: neither was it he that hated me that did magnify himself against me; then I would have hid myself from him: (13) But it was thou, a man mine equal, my guide, and mine acquaintance. (14) We took sweet counsel together, and walked unto the house of God in company. *(Psalm 55:12-14)*

"As unknown, and yet well known…" *(2 Corinthians 6:9)*. In the ministry there are unsung heroes just laboring for God in the background with no need of recognition, while others are and must be out in front leading. There is no doubt in my mind that some of the greatest Christians are behind the scenes simply laboring in prayer and fasting for the work of God.

"…as dying, and, behold, we live…" *(2 Corinthians 6:9)*. Praise the LORD we will all live forever even though we pass through the valley of death from mortal to immortal!

"…as chastened, and not killed" *(2 Corinthians 6:9)*. All of God's born-again children will one time or another fall into the chastening hand of Almighty God. In Psalm 38:1, 2, we see the plea of David as he fell under the chastening hand of God: "(1) O LORD, rebuke me not in thy wrath: neither chasten me in thy hot displeasure. (2) For thine arrows stick fast in me, and thy hand presseth me sore." In Spurgeon's *Treasury of David*, he makes this comment about these verses: "Chasten me if thou wilt, it is a Father's prerogative, and to endure it obediently is a child's duty; but, O turn not the rod into a sword, smite not so as to kill." [20]

"As sorrowful, yet alway rejoicing; as poor, yet making many rich; as having nothing, and yet possessing all things" *(2 Corinthians 6:10)*. Finally, we are able to rejoice with the LORD in all things. We may be poor on this earth, but as we introduce men to Christ, they will become joint heirs with Christ sharing His riches for eternity! What a Saviour!

In the closing statements of the *Heartbeats of the Holy*, Keith Knauss made these comments that sum up the call, the hardships, and the duty of a preacher:

> What are temporary toils and trials, and brief battles with the bulls of Bashan, when weighed against the pleasures forevermore at God's right hand? One moment in the presence with Him Who has called us with a Holy calling will more than compensate for the inconveniences and impediments of the passing present.
>
> Let us then lay aside all the unnecessary, and preach! Preach the Word! Preach the Cross and Christ! Preach faithfully in season and out! Preach on and on, "Looking unto Jesus the Author and Finisher of our faith; Who for the JOY...Endured...!" [21]

We all want God's approval for our ministry. Fasting is included in the formula the Apostle Paul listed for us under the inspiration of the blessed Holy Ghost. Some of the fasts that Paul endured were quite possibly due to the fact that he had no food. Others were due to his work habits or his mourning. The psalmist said this: "My heart is smitten, and withered like grass; so that I forget to eat my bread" *(Psalm 102:4)*. Some people get so involved in their work they either do not think about eating or simply do not take the time to eat. There is also no doubt in my mind that the apostle Paul set time aside to humble himself before his Holy God in the art of fasting!

In the next chapters, we will dissect this topic and, by God's grace, will help you to understand the importance of including fasting in your life.

"The question can be posed—How serious are you about your desire to have God hear and answer your prayer."

CHAPTER TWO

DIFFERENT TYPES
Of Fasting

The Absolute Fast is when you do not eat or drink water. Queen Esther displayed this fast for us: "Go, gather together all the Jews that are present in Shushan, and fast ye for me, and neither eat nor drink three days, night or day…" *(Esther 4:16)*. We see here the exact amount of time and the precise instructions to not eat or drink anything. This fast was one of great urgency! Not only was Mordecai's life and the entire Jewish race in danger, but Esther, too, was a Jew and in jeopardy of execution.

There is great power in corporate prayer and fasting. This is obvious when we read the outcome of this wonderful display of fasting coupled with prayer. The question can be posed, how serious are you about your desire to have God hear and answer your request?

We also see this fast practiced by Paul directly after his conversion: "And he was three days without sight, and neither did eat nor drink" *(Acts 9:9)*. In today's world God is not knocking people over and speaking directly to them in an audible voice from Heaven. If so, we would probably see more people concerned about what God would have them do for the rest of their lives. Today, faith is the element needed for salvation, separation, and service. Paul was so overwhelmed by God's saving grace that he wanted to know His perfect will for his life. Due to his legalistic belief, he was no stranger to fasting, but now he exercised fasting to fall completely into God's will. A preacher once said, we need to "fall asleep in the will of God!" This is the greatest advice one could ever receive and incorporate into his life!

It was evident that Paul was in fear for his life: "And he trembling and astonished said, LORD, what wilt thou have me to do? And the LORD said unto him, Arise, and go into the city, and it shall be told thee what thou must do" *(Acts 9:6)*. Oh that man would fear Almighty God today and seek Him in prayer and fasting to find His perfect will for his life!

Ezra, as an act of mourning, also exercised the Absolute

Fast: Then Ezra rose up from before the house of God, and went into the chamber of Johanan the son of Eliashib: and when he came thither, he did eat no bread, nor drink water: for he mourned because of the transgression of them that had been carried away. *(Ezra 10:6)*

The Absolute Fast is definitely one that is exercised during a time of great need or sorrow. With this discipline, you will get the attention of God in a powerful way. Again, you will not back God into a corner causing Him to answer your request the way you want, but you will give God the liberty to answer your prayer in the way He wants! You will have peace that He knows best, and He will give you the grace to endure the answer.

The Water-Only Fast or Complete Fast is when you do not eat, but you drink water. The LORD Jesus Christ displayed this fast for us: "Being forty days tempted of the devil. And in those days he did eat nothing: and when they were ended, he afterward hungered" *(Luke 4:2)*. This verse reveals to us that Christ did not eat anything, but it does not say that he did not drink. If this were true, the Bible would have said that He was not only hungry but thirsty, also. From a physical reality, one cannot go without water very long.

The Water-Only Fast is quite possibly the fast most commonly known among Christians. There is a great need to make Christians aware of the other types of fasting recorded for us in God's Word. There are many ways to fast, and no doubt there is one that will meet your physical limitations, too.

The Normal Fast is one that is probably the most practiced. In this fast, you do not eat any solid food but rather drink juices or vitamin drinks for a period of time you determine. One or two days seem to be the length commonly practiced.

The Supernatural Fast is illustrated for us in the Bible by Moses' eighty-day fast with no food or water: "When I was gone up into the mount to receive the tables of stone, even the tables of the covenant which the LORD made with you, then I abode in the mount forty days and forty nights, I neither did eat bread nor drink water" *(Deuteronomy 9:9)*. During this time, God delivered to Moses the two tables of stone with the Ten Commandments written with His finger. After the forty-day period was up, God told Moses to go down to the people because they had fallen into deep sin. God told Moses that He wanted to destroy the people for their wickedness! When Moses arrived, he threw the tables of stone to the ground breaking them in pieces, fell on his face before God, and entered into another forty-day fast eating no food and drinking no water: "And I fell down before the LORD, as at the first, forty days and forty nights: I did neither eat bread, nor drink water, because of all your sins which ye sinned, in doing wickedly in the sight of the LORD, to provoke him to anger" *(Deuteronomy 9:18).*

In verse 14, we see God angered by the sins of the people and saying to Moses, "Let me alone, that I may destroy them, and blot out their name from under heaven: and I will make of thee a nation mightier and greater than they" *(Deuteronomy 9:14).* Moses was given an opportunity by God to be made the leader of a nation of people that would be superior, but he chose to humble himself on behalf of his friends and family and cry out to God for mercy for them in another Supernatural Fast. There is no possible explanation other than supernatural involvement from God to allow Moses to fast for eighty straight days. This is the longest recorded fast in our Bible.

Elijah also experienced a forty-day Supernatural Fast when he was fed by an angel and went on a forty-day journey without any other food.

(7) And the angel of the LORD came again the second time, and touched him, and said, Arise and eat; because the journey is too great for thee. (8) And he arose, and did eat and drink, and went in the strength of that meat forty days and forty nights unto Horeb the mount of God.
(1 Kings 19:7, 8)

This verse does seem to suggest that he did not drink either, but really there is no way of knowing this for sure. The Bible says that he went in the strength of the meat but makes no mention of drink. It is highly probable that he did not drink either but went fully in the strength given him by the angel of the LORD.

There is a great resemblance between Elijah and Moses. As we have seen, both of them experienced the Supernatural Fast that can only be explained by direct intervention of our Holy God. Both had supernatural endings of their lives. Moses is recorded as dying but having God bury him:

(5) So Moses the servant of the LORD died there in the land of Moab, according to the word of the LORD. (6) And he buried him in a valley in the land of Moab, over against Bethpeor: but no man knoweth of his sepulchre unto this day. *(Deuteronomy 34:5, 6)*

Elijah was taken by God in a whirlwind: "And it came to pass, as they still went on, and talked, that, behold, there appeared a chariot of fire, and horses of fire, and parted them both asunder; and Elijah went up by a whirlwind into heaven" *(2 Kings 2:11)*. Both of these men reappeared with Christ on the mountain: "And, behold, there appeared unto them Moses and Elias talking with him" *(Matthew 17:3)*. Both of these men had a supernatural touch of God; Moses was chosen to be the one who presented God's Law to the people, and Elijah was the one God used in the restoration process of the Law.

> (4) Remember ye the law of Moses my servant, which I commanded unto him in Horeb for all Israel, with the statutes and judgments. (5) Behold, I will send you Elijah the prophet before the coming of the great and dreadful day of the LORD: (6) And he shall turn the heart of the fathers to the children, and the heart of the children to their fathers, lest I come and smite the earth with a curse. *(Malachi 4:4-6)*

The Partial Fast is abstaining from pleasure or from certain foods. This fast is recorded for us in the story of Daniel and his three friends, Hananiah, Mishael, and Azariah, when they would not defile themselves with the king's meat: "And put a knife to thy throat, if thou be a man given to appetite" *(Proverbs 23:2)*. Daniel did not want to eat the food prepared for the king for a couple of reasons. First, the meat may have been offered to false gods; and second, it was food that was not healthy for the body. His request was to prove that the Jewish diet provided by their God was much better than the one their captors were offering.

> (12) Prove thy servants, I beseech thee, ten days; and let them give us pulse to eat, and water to drink. (13) Then let our countenances be looked upon before thee, and the countenance of the children that eat of the portion of the king's meat: and as thou seest, deal with thy servants. *(Daniel 1:12)*

His fast worked, and he was granted his request to eat the food of his choice. We know God used these four men in a great way. Daniel's loyalty to God caused the king to declare his God as the one true God.

> (25) Then king Darius wrote unto all people, nations, and languages, that dwell in all the earth; Peace be multiplied unto you. (26) I make a decree, That in every dominion of my kingdom men tremble and fear before the God of Daniel: for

he is the living God, and stedfast for ever, and his kingdom that which shall not be destroyed, and his dominion shall be even unto the end. *(Daniel 6:25, 26)*

We see the fast from a certain pleasure demonstrated by King Darius when Daniel was thrown into the lion's den: "Then the king went to his palace, and passed the night fasting: neither were instruments of musick brought before him: and his sleep went from him" *(Daniel 6:18)*. In this passage the king fasted, not only from food, but also from any pleasure. He did not allow music to be played in his presence, nor did he sleep. This allowed King Darius to stay focused on the need at hand and to diligently pray: "...The effectual fervent prayer of a righteous man availeth much" *(James 5:16)*. It is quite possible the King Darius learned this practice by observing his servant Daniel during some of his seasons of fasting. When you are willing to give up something that you enjoy as a reminder to pray, it will amaze you how many times you remember to pray for your request.

Fasting from sleep is also very difficult. Your body needs sleep and water to exist; it can survive for a long period of time without food, but it takes supernatural intervention to survive extended periods of time without sleep and water. Pastor Lynn Janie says, "When you run out of the natural, try the supernatural!"

In spite of what you may think of former President George W. Bush, I believe he is a born-again Christian. In the book *The Man in the Middle*, by Timothy S. Goeglein, President Bush gives a clear answer concerning his salvation:

> The comfortability factor really rose for President Bush among social conservatives dating from his answer in that December 14, 1999 Iowa Republican Primary debate when he was asked who his favorite philosopher was. Succinctly, and without pause, Bush answered "Christ because He changed my heart." [22]

Timothy Goeglein testified of many occasions he witnessed President Bush praying. According to his book, "He was a man of prayer and faith. I was honored and humbled to pray with him on several occasions in the Oval Office and elsewhere." [23]

In the book *The Faith of George W. Bush*, by Stephen Mansfield, it is recorded that President Bush also was a man that believed in fasting. President Bush had been actively trying to restore a faith in God in the executive branch before the terrorist attack on our country. According to Mansfield:

The secular state seemed to recede for a time. Congressional leaders sang hymns on the Capitol steps and even introduced legislation to adopt "God Bless America" as the official national hymn.

What followed was a freer reign for religion in American society. Bush seemed to embody it. He prayed publicly and spoke of faith, divine destiny, and the nation's religious heritage more than he ever had. Aids found him facedown on the floor in prayer in the Oval Office. It became known that he refused to eat sweets while American troops were in Iraq, a partial fast seldom reported of an American president.
24

Regardless of what you think of President George W. Bush, Mr. Bush knew how to get ahold of the God of Heaven with his requests! We can thank God that we had a Godly President in office during the most tragic time in America's history since the Japanese bombed Pearl Harbor! Our borders have been safe from major terrorist activity because our leader prayed and fasted. Thank God he had enough concern for our troops, while they were in harm's way keeping America safe, to deprive himself of the simple pleasure of eating sweets. There is no doubt our Commander-in-Chief, during his eight-year term in office and to this day, prays regularly for our armed forces.

Limiting your diet to certain foods can be considered as a Partial Fast: "Prove thy servants, I beseech thee, ten days; and let them give us pulse to eat, and water to drink" *(Daniel 1:12)*. I preached on fasting in a church in Illinois a few years back. I am always careful to explain the Partial Fast so people can understand that, regardless of your health situation, there is something you can fast from to enhance your prayers. A dear elderly lady approached me with tears in her eyes. She told me she had a lost son, and she knew what she could fast from. She understood two things: first, there is power in adding fasting to your prayers; and second, God will show you what to fast from and for how long. The question once again arises, how serious are you?

To sum up a Partial Fast, anything that brings you pleasure can be abstained from as a fast. I laugh remembering a young man in a juvenile facility who told me he was going to fast from cussing!

Any of these above fasts will be recognized by God when they are done in such a fashion that you are not drawing attention to yourself, but you are humbling yourself before the Almighty God. In today's busy lifestyle, it would be next to impossible to go on an extended fast without being noticed, but there is a difference between broadcasting the information for public recognition and someone noticing that you are fasting. You will experience significant weight loss during an extended fast. Some may be concerned about your health and continue to ask you questions. If this persists simply tell them that you are perfectly healthy and are in the middle of a fast. Leave it at that, and, hopefully, they will pray for you and allow you your solitude. Many times, as a preacher, I shared the table with other preachers and friends during my fast. I would tell them that I am not eating today. Do not tell them that you are not hungry but that you are not eating. Most Christians will recognize you are fasting and help you to feel comfortable at the table.

The Bible gives clear instruction for a Partial Fast that is shared by a married couple, too.

> (4) The wife hath not power of her own body, but the husband: and likewise also the husband hath not power of his own body, but the wife. (5) Defraud ye not one the other, except it be with consent for a time, that ye may give yourselves to fasting and prayer; and come together again, that Satan tempt you not for your incontinency. *(1 Corinthians 7:4, 5)*

There are no hard-core rules and regulations for fasting, but the LORD does give us avenues to tap into His full power source. Husbands and wives often have needs that demand God's full attention, and fasting is one way of getting it. If both parties consent, then abstaining from marital relations can also be implemented into the fast. Notice the benefit from this practice is that God will hinder Satan from tempting you. The word *incontinency* has the meaning of not being able to restrain your passion. If you and your wife are unable to abstain for a brief time, it could mean that Satan will tempt you. This does not imply that you will fall into the temptation, but any temptation that you do not have to endure is one fewer into which you may fall!

As you can see, there are many types of fasting in the Bible. Seek the LORD for direction, choose the one that best fits you, and begin to tap into God's power. When you begin to develop a life of fasting, you will be plugging into a very powerful resource God has made available to His children.

"Prayer without fasting is like sitting behind the wheel of a sports car with a thousand-horse power and never turning on the ignition."

CHAPTER THREE

MYTHS & REASONS WHY
Fasting Is Not Being Practiced

One reason for the absence of fasting is the lack of instruction on the subject. It seems as if the topic of fasting has been avoided from the pulpits of Independent Baptists. It is possible that fasting has not been taught from the pulpit for a number of reasons. First, there is no doubt that Biblical fasting is not widely practiced. There are great men and women who have practiced fasting for years and continue to do so, but, for some reason, it is simply avoided in the pulpits. There are preachers in our movement that see no need to fast. Again, this can be blamed on lack of instruction on the topic. If a young Christian does not know how, when, or why to fast, what makes us think he will be able to instruct others about it? The end result is trapped power. It is like sitting behind the wheel of a sports car with a thousand-horse power and never turning on the ignition.

It seems like our Bible colleges are graduating career men of God who know the ins and outs of ministry but know very little about how to tap into the powerful resources God has stored for our use. The difference between a man of God and a great man of God is the touch of God. A touch of God cannot be instructed in a classroom but can be obtained during a meeting with Him in humility and prayer. I preached a message entitled "*God's Approval on Your Ministry*" in one of our fundamental Bible colleges. Not too long after, I received this note in an email from a student who was about to graduate and start a church:

> Up until now, I have depended on what I can do through the books that I have read and the methods I have learned in starting this church. But I have realized that unless the LORD build the church, I will be laboring in vain, trying to build it myself. What I need is that time alone with God, fasting and praying for God's power and hand upon me as I try and do a work for Him. So, I am looking forward to studying out this subject of fasting.

Our fundamental Bible colleges are doing an outstanding job

training our young men and ladies for ministry. There is no doubt that the topic of fasting does surface in the instructional time but could probably be expounded on more.

It is essential that we declare the glory of God and brag on the power that comes from fasting. One of the biggest myths concerning fasting is that you should never talk about your experience. This conclusion is drawn because of the teachings of Christ concerning fasting. When Jesus is teaching about fasting in Matthew chapter 6, He is saying that during your fast you should not appear unto men to be fasting. This could bring glory to you instead of the LORD:

> (16) Moreover when ye fast, be not, as the hypocrites, of a sad countenance: for they disfigure their faces, that they may appear unto men to fast. Verily I say unto you, They have their reward. (17) But thou, when thou fastest, anoint thine head, and wash thy face; (18) That thou appear not unto men to fast, but unto thy Father which is in secret: and thy Father, which seeth in secret, shall reward thee openly. *(Matthew 6: 16-18)*

During your fast, it is not appropriate to speak of your fast so you can look as if you are some kind of spiritual giant. Your fast will go unrecognized by the LORD if you choose to have the praise of men: "They have their reward."

On the other hand, the LORD tells us many times to proclaim His wonderful works. We need to tell the results of our fasting to others so they, too, will have the desire to meet with the LORD through fasting. You will not lose favor or reward with the LORD when you brag on the method He chose to complete your communication with Him. One of the greatest men of prayer of our time told me that fasting was a very private part of his life that he chose not to talk about. He was missing out on sharing the marvelous power of God he has personally experienced through fasting. Who could tell how God would use his testimonies about fasting? Do not be afraid to brag on God!

Here are some of the verses that tell us that we need to proclaim His wondrous works:

> Sing unto him, sing psalms unto him, talk ye of all his wondrous works. *(1 Chronicles 16:9)*

> Declare his glory among the heathen; his marvellous works among all nations. *(1 Chronicles 16:24)*

> That I may publish with the voice of thanksgiving, and tell

of all thy wondrous works. *(Psalm 26:7)*

Many, O LORD my God, are thy wonderful works which thou hast done, and thy thoughts which are to us-ward: they cannot be reckoned up in order unto thee: if I would declare and speak of them, they are more than can be numbered. *(Psalm 40:5)*

O God, thou hast taught me from my youth: and hitherto have I declared thy wondrous works. *(Psalm 71:17)*

But it is good for me to draw near to God: I have put my trust in the LORD GOD, that I may declare all thy works. *(Psalm 73:28)*

We will not hide them from their children, shewing to the generation to come the praises of the LORD, and his strength, and his wonderful works that he hath done. *(Psalm 78:4)*

Declare his glory among the heathen, his wonders among all people. *(Psalm 96:3)*

(1) O give thanks unto the LORD; call upon his name: make known his deeds among the people. (2) Sing unto him, sing psalms unto him: talk ye of all his wondrous works. *(Psalm 105:1, 2)*

And let them sacrifice the sacrifices of thanksgiving, and declare his works with rejoicing. *(Psalm 107:22)*

He hath made his wonderful works to be remembered: the LORD is gracious and full of compassion. *(Psalm 111:4)*

I shall not die, but live, and declare the works of the LORD. *(Psalm 118:17)*

Make me to understand the way of thy precepts: so shall I talk of thy wondrous works. *(Psalm 119:27)*

(4) One generation shall praise thy works to another, and shall declare thy mighty acts. (5) I will speak of the glorious honour of thy majesty, and of thy wondrous works. *(Psalm 145:4, 5)*

Cretes and Arabians, we do hear them speak in our tongues the wonderful works of God. *(Acts 2:11)*

People are more apt to communicate with God through fasting if they know it is working for others.

And all men shall fear, and shall declare the work of God; for they shall wisely consider of his doing. *(Psalm 64:9)*

Come and hear, all ye that fear God, and I will declare what he hath done for my soul. *(Psalm 66:16)*

Another myth concerning fasting is the element of hunger during your fast. I have had the privilege to counsel with many youth pastors during my years of working with juveniles. I will never forget one occasion when I was encouraging a young man to fast for his youth department. He told me that I did not understand; he went on to inform me that every time he tried to fast he got really hungry! Hunger is a part of fasting!

Every once in a while you will cross paths with someone who will tell you if your fast is God-called, you will not even feel hungry or weak. That person is probably much more spiritual than I; I was hungry and weak during almost all of my fasting. So was the psalmist: "My knees are weak through fasting; and my flesh faileth of fatness" *(Psalm 109:24)*. You will experience weakness, headaches from a withdrawal of caffeine, and, naturally, you will lose weight. You can function and perform a regular schedule on an extended fast. You must ask the LORD for victory, and He will give it to you. There are times after three or four days that your hunger pains will subside, but my personal experiences involved hunger.

When we read the account of the woman at the well in John chapter 4, we see the unconditional love Christ has for sinners. He knew her sin and was willing to talk with her even though she was a Gentile. When the disciples arrived back on the scene with food for Christ and compelled Him to eat, He informed them: "...I have meat to eat that ye know not of" *(John 4:32)*. Because of this statement, the disciples thought someone had brought Him some food: "Therefore said the disciples one to another, Hath any man brought him ought to eat?" *(John 4:33)*. What they did not realize was that even though Christ had not taken any physical meat, he was being sustained by spiritual meat. God will give us the strength to do His work in His power when we are in His perfect will. We go in His strength during this time of physical weakness. In essence, we are denying ourselves of physical nourishment and replacing it with spiritual nourishment.

Each one of my extended fasts was during my regular scheduled activities. I traveled thousands of miles, preached many messages, conducted many revival meetings in juvenile institutions, worked in my yard, worked on my car, played with my children, along with any other activity that needed my attention. I did not work as hard or fast, and I did require more rest than normal, but I did keep a regular schedule.

Cults and false religions have robbed us of the power of fasting too. Fasting is a religious practice that many cults employ. This does not mean that we cannot practice fasting in our faith. God intended for us to fast, not necessarily commanding us but expecting us to fast. This is why He said, "Moreover when ye fast, be not, as the hypocrites, of a sad countenance: for they disfigure their faces, that they may appear unto men to fast. Verily I say unto you, They have their reward" *(Matthew 6:16)*. The LORD Jesus made the statement "…when ye fast…" knowing that it will take place in the Christian life. He was also very careful to explain to the disciples the reason they could not cast out the demon from the young lad: "Howbeit this kind goeth not out but by prayer and fasting" *(Matthew 17:21)*. The truth is, fasting coupled with prayer can and will produce the power needed to accomplish great things in your ministry, including the means to resist a demonic attack. I will be talking more about this in the upcoming pages.

Fasting is a wonderful way to spend personal time with the LORD! There are many reasons why people have not included fasting in their spiritual walks. I hope to help you get a glimpse of what God has taught me through studying and practicing each of these fasts so you, too, can begin to implement this in your arsenal of weapons for the ministry.

The best instruction a child receives will come from his parents! "Train up a child in the way he should go: and when he is old, he will not depart from it."

(PROVERBS 22:6)

CHAPTER FOUR

TEACH YOUR CHILDREN
to Prepare for Spiritual Warfare

"For we wrestle not against flesh and blood, but against principalities, against powers, against the rulers of the darkness of this world, against spiritual wickedness in high places" *(Ephesians 6:12)*. Any Christian who decides to answer the call to be a servant of the King will face many battles that demand preparation. The Apostle Paul gives us a list of tactics to prepare ourselves for this battle: "Wherefore take unto you the whole armour of God, that ye may be able to withstand in the evil day, and having done all, to stand" *(Ephesians 6:13)*. Once we have learned how to use each weapon in the mighty arsenal, then it is our responsibility to ensure that the future generation of Christian warriors is girded with the whole armor of God, which includes fasting.

Right from the beginning the devil attacked the Word of God and has been doing so ever since. The LORD has preserved for us His Word in the King James Bible. Here is an example of how the devil has removed a few words that have stripped the truth from many believers who do not use the King James Bible. This is a quote from Richard W. De Haan, the late M. R. De Haan's son concerning Mark 9:29: "The words ('and fasting' which occur in our King James Version are not found in the best Greek manuscripts. Furthermore, there would have been no opportunity for the disciples to fast in connection with their attempts to heal this boy.)" [25]

Many of the new versions of the Bible, translated from what is referred to as "the best Greek manuscripts," have removed the words "and fasting." The removal of this phrase alone is robbing the readers of the valuable teaching of this powerful Biblical principal. What Richard De Haan did not understand is fasting prepares you for the upcoming battles as well as the ones that may currently involve you!

Jesus was a man, God in flesh and our earthly example. He practiced fasting on many different occasions. We know that He started His earthly ministry with a forty-day water-only fast: "And when he had fasted forty days and forty nights, he was afterward an hungred" *(Matthew 4:2)*. When He was approached by His disciples at the well, He told them that He had meat to eat that they knew not of: "(31) In the meanwhile his disciples prayed him, saying, Master, eat. (32) But he said unto them, I have meat to eat that ye know not of" (John 4:31, 32). Jesus was not referring to physical food, but He was speaking of heavenly nourishment as he refrained from physical food to rescue the poor lost sinner at the well. We also know that He was willing to leave His heavenly home to become sin for us. Separation from His Father and the heavenly host for thirty-three and one-half years was also a form of fasting.

"Howbeit this kind goeth not out but by prayer and fasting" *(Matthew 17:21)*. In this passage of Scripture, Jesus was teaching His disciples that they, too, needed to realize that they must prepare for spiritual battles in the future. They would not always have Christ with them in person to help them. This situation was Christ's way of teaching His disciples, and the future Christian army, that fasting is a necessary tool in fighting spiritual warfare.

Fasting is a Biblical way to tap into the power of God in preparation for upcoming battles. Many times great men of God have fasted and prayed before meetings or before attempting to do a work for God. Once again, it shows the LORD that you are serious enough about what you are trying to accomplish to abstain from physical food in order to receive His power and approval to accomplish the task at hand.

Dr. Gearis, former president and co-founder of Rock of Ages Prison Ministry, made this statement concerning extended fasting: "Do it while you are young; when you get old and sick, you will not be able to fast."

As you study the topic of fasting, you will notice that the number *nine* is used to reference many verses on the subject. In Deuteronomy 9:9, we see the longest recorded fast by Moses; in Acts 9:9, Paul fasted three days and nights; in Nehemiah 9:1, Israel assembled with fastings; in Daniel 9:3, Daniel fasted for his nation; in Matthew 9:14, 15, Jesus taught on fasting; in Psalm 109:24, the psalmist described his physical ailments during his fasting; in Zechariah 8:19, the LORD set in motion specific fasts; in Mark 9:29, Jesus said, "And he said unto them, This kind can come forth by nothing, but by prayer and fasting."

As a student of the Bible, you know that numerology plays a very important role in your studies. A brief study of the number *nine* gives us an insight to the significance of the use of this number in so many references in the Bible concerning fasting. In the book *Numbers in the Bible* by Robert D. Johnston, one of the definitions of number *nine* is the fruit of the Spirit; but there is another definition that brings to light the value of fasting:

> This is the last of those single numerals known as digits, beyond which we have merely combinations of those previous digits. It, therefore, marks the end. It is the number of finality or judgment. But nine is also three times three, and three signifies Divine completeness. Hence nine denotes finality in Divine things.[26]

Finality or the final action of seeking the LORD for a specific request can be fasting. It could be stated that your prayer life is not complete until you fast! It is like getting both ears of God during your prayer time, or, in essence, how serious are you?

Teaching your children to add fasting to their prayers can and will introduce them to divine completeness in their prayer lives. We have the example of a young person learning this valuable lesson in the pages of the book of Esther.

> (13) And the letters were sent by posts into all the king's provinces, to destroy, to kill, and to cause to perish, all Jews, both young and old, little children and women, in one day, even upon the thirteenth day of the twelfth month, which is the month Adar, and to take the spoil of them for a prey. (14) The copy of the writing for a commandment to be given in every province was published unto all people, that they should be ready against that day. *(Esther 3: 13, 14)*

We see in these verses that a decree to destroy the Jewish people was sent out by "...this wicked Haman..." *(Esther 7:6)*. It is interesting how the number *six* denotes the manifestation of evil and is the number given for man. Number six is one number short of perfection. *Seven* is the number that indicates perfection; therefore, the number given to man, *six*, is just missing Christ who makes man complete in the eyes of God. Without Christ, man is incomplete, lost, and undone. Haman had devised a plan to destroy all of the Jews and convinced King Ahasuerus to sign a writing to destroy them: "To destroy, to kill, and to cause to perish, all Jews, both young and old, little children and women, in one day, even upon the thirteenth day of the twelfth month, which is the month Adar, and to take the spoil of them for a prey" *(Esther 3:13)*. When the Jewish people read this decree, which had been posted in every province, they surely began to pray to the God of their fathers for help. In chapter 4 of the book of Esther, we even see Mordecai with his clothes rent, dressed in sackcloth and ashes, and crying bitterly in the midst of the city. "When Mordecai perceived all that was done, Mordecai rent his clothes, and put on sackcloth with ashes, and went out into the midst of the city, and cried with a loud and a bitter cry" *(Esther 4:1).* Sackcloth and ashes is an outward demonstration of mourning. It seemed as if, due to the great trial he was facing, he forgot how to reach out to God.

Notice how Esther prepared for her entrance into the king's chamber when she decided to accept the challenge of approaching him with her request. First of all, in chapter 4, verse 11, you will see that an uninvited appearance before the king was an appointment with death. What she failed to realize is that she was married to the king and could have boldly approached the throne. Praise the LORD that we can come before Him with our requests. We have been born in, adopted in, and married in! Glory!

> (15) For we have not an high priest which cannot be touched with the feeling of our infirmities; but was in all points tempted like as we are, yet without sin. (16) Let us therefore come boldly unto the throne of grace, that we may obtain mercy, and find grace to help in time of need. *(Hebrews 4:15, 16)*

Esther knew she must have the help of our Holy God to intervene in her case. Notice her preparation for the gigantic task that was ahead of her. She commanded Mordecai to…

> Go, gather together all the Jews that are present in Shushan, and fast ye for me, and neither eat nor drink three days, night or day: I also and my maidens will fast likewise; and so will I go in unto the king, which is not according to the law: and if I perish, I perish. *(Esther 4:16)*

Did you notice that she did not say, "fast and pray." Esther was sure that the people were already praying. Some were even fasting (4:3), but she wanted all of the Jews to collectively fast for their people. This demonstrates to us that fasting is a totally separate way to reach God with our requests! Again, fasting gets both ears of our God (FINALITY IN DIVINE THINGS)! It is like sitting behind the wheel of the sports car I mentioned earlier, but this time with the engine running and your foot to the floor in full acceleration!

How did she know what to do in such a time of crisis? This can be answered from the Scripture: "Esther had not yet shewed her kindred nor her people; as Mordecai had charged her: for Esther did the commandment of Mordecai, like as when she was brought up with him" *(Esther 2:20).* Esther was raised in the home of Mordecai: "And he brought up Hadassah, that is, Esther, his uncle's daughter: for she had neither father nor mother, and the maid was fair and beautiful; whom Mordecai, when her father and mother were dead, took for his own daughter" *(Esther 2:7).*

Mordecai was her cousin and a man who feared God. The whole reason the Jews were in this mess was due to the fact that Mordecai would not bow down to the wicked Haman because of Mordecai's respect for God's commandments: "Thou shalt not bow down thyself to them, nor serve them: for I the LORD thy God am a jealous God, visiting the iniquity of the fathers upon the children unto the third and fourth generation of them that hate me" *(Exodus 20:5).* When tough times arose in Mordecai's home, there is no doubt he would gather the family together and proclaim a fast. God is not a liar! He honored their fasting and answered their prayers. Esther was raised in a home that practiced getting ahold of God through fasting. This concept can be proved by the procedure she chose to use when approaching the king. When Esther prepared spiritually for a task that would determine the destiny of God's chosen people, she must have recalled her training as a child: "...Esther did the commandment of Mordecai, like as when she was brought up with him" *(Esther 2:20).* She knew exactly what to do and how to do it because of her instruction in fasting. She reminded Mordecai of this when she commanded him to gather the people together and fast. Mordecai must have thought to himself, *Why didn't I think of that!* Sometimes we need to be reminded of the way God wants us to act in time of trouble.

It is very important to teach our children these valuable techniques of meeting with God while they are young. It is essential not only to share prayer requests with your children but also to share with them God's answer. They must see and know God is at work in your lives through prayer coupled with fasting!

As the story continues, Esther invited the king to a banquet where she would share her request: "And the king said unto Esther at the banquet of wine, What is thy petition? and it shall be granted thee: and what is thy request? even to the half of the kingdom it shall be performed" *(Esther 5:6).* After a series of events, Haman was exposed and suffered the consequence for his evil ways. Esther's request was granted by the king, Mordecai was honored for being loyal to the king, Haman was hung on the gallows he built to hang Mordecai, and the Jews were spared.

Queen Esther had a godly influence in her life that instructed her in Biblical ways to seek God in time of trouble. It is our responsibility to teach the next generation this great and powerful way to communicate with our LORD, too.

> (19) And ye shall teach them your children, speaking of them when thou sittest in thine house, and when thou walkest by the way, when thou liest down, and when thou risest up. (20) And thou shalt write them upon the door posts of thine house, and upon thy gates: (21) That your days may be multiplied, and the days of your children, in the land which the LORD sware unto your fathers to give them, as the days of heaven upon the earth. (22) For if ye shall diligently keep all these commandments which I command you, to do them, to love the LORD your God, to walk in all his ways, and to cleave unto him; (23) Then will the LORD drive out all these nations from before you, and ye shall possess greater nations and mightier than yourselves. *(Deuteronomy 11:19-23)*

Christ has given us His example during the beginning phases of His earthly ministry. He chose to robe Himself in flesh and to endure all as a man so we could learn from His example. As mentioned before, the first thing Christ did in preparation for His earthly ministry was to enter into a forty-day water-only fast:

> (1) Then was Jesus led up of the Spirit into the wilderness to be tempted of the devil. (2) And when he had fasted forty days and forty nights, he was afterward an hungred. *(Matthew 4:1, 2)*

This is a very difficult fast; but when you are finished, you will have God's direction in your life. This must be a fast that God calls you to do. Seek Him in prayer asking for a Scripture before you begin. It is also a good idea to seek counsel from your medical doctor before you begin. He will have some advice that you may consider, but, remember, it will be the power of God that will sustain you. Please note that some medical doctors, unless they are Christian doctors, may not understand extended fasting. This would be a good time to witness to them and share with them the power God has in store for those who follow His instructions.

What a fantastic way to train your children to seek God's will for their lives! Most Christians wander in life not knowing the will of God in their lives. There are many examples given to Christians in His Word, but if the Christian warrior does not take the whole armor, the enemy will soon defeat him.

It is estimated by Dr. J. Harold Smith that there are eighty-six references in the Word of God that speak of fasting.[27] With this many references to fasting in the Bible, it is certain the LORD wants us to practice fasting. Fasting has not been outdated! Dr. Smith makes this recommendation: "Go on a hunger strike for the glory of God."[28]

"You are not going to back God into a corner and force Him to answer your prayer the way you desire, but you are giving God the liberty to move in your life the way He pleases."

CHAPTER FIVE

LENGTHS
of Fasts

There are no set guidelines for the amount of time or the type of fast. As we have seen, there are different types of fasts that do give specific instructions (Esther Fast), but the one that God chooses for you is personal: "Is not this the fast that I have chosen? to loose the bands of wickedness, to undo the heavy burdens, and to let the oppressed go free, and that ye break every yoke?" *(Isaiah 58:6).* Be sure you seek the LORD for direction in your fasting.

A good recommendation is that you begin with a twenty-four hour fast. If you eat a meal at noon one day then break your fast at one o'clock the next, you will have completed a full twenty-four hour period, and you will basically miss two meals. As the LORD leads, you can go into longer fasts or, by all means, if He calls you directly into an extended fast, go for it! He is no respecter of persons and will give you strength and peace beyond your imagination. It is highly recommended that you consult your doctor first, especially if you are on some type of medication. There is no place in the Bible where God directed a man into a fast that physically injured or killed him.

As we discussed in the previous chapter, Moses completed the longest recorded fast in the Bible when he did two forty-day fasts back to back. This was definitely a supernatural fast.

One-day fasts were very common in the Bible and can become a part of your worship to the LORD. You can pick one day a week, or month, to fast for a particular reason, or God may call you to fast for an urgent matter. Here are some examples:

> And they gathered together to Mizpeh, and drew water, and poured it out before the LORD, and fasted on that day, and said there, We have sinned against the LORD. And Samuel judged the children of Israel in Mizpeh. *(1 Samuel 7:6)*

> So Jonathan arose from the table in fierce anger, and did eat no meat the second day of the month: for he was grieved for David, because his father had done him shame. *(I Samuel 20:34)*

Then Saul fell straightway all along on the earth, and was sore afraid, because of the words of Samuel: and there was no strength in him; for he had eaten no bread all the day, nor all the night. *(1 Samuel 28:20)*

And when all the people came to cause David to eat meat while it was yet day, David sware, saying, So do God to me, and more also, if I taste bread, or ought else, till the sun be down. *(2 Samuel 3:35)*

Three-day fasts were also observed as we have already discussed in the Esther fast: "Go, gather together all the Jews that are present in Shushan, and fast ye for me, and neither eat nor drink three days, night or day..." *(Esther 4:16)*. This is a fast for a matter of great urgency!

Seven-day fasts are recorded also: "And they took their bones, and buried them under a tree at Jabesh, and fasted seven days" *(1 Samuel 31:13)*. David is seen fasting seven days for his sick child and ends his fast when he hears news of the child's death.

(16) David therefore besought God for the child; and David fasted, and went in, and lay all night upon the earth. (17) And the elders of his house arose, and went to him, to raise him up from the earth: but he would not, neither did he eat bread with them. (18) And it came to pass on the seventh day, that the child died. And the servants of David feared to tell him that the child was dead: for they said, Behold, while the child was yet alive, we spake unto him, and he would not hearken unto our voice: how will he then vex himself, if we tell him that the child is dead? (19) But when David saw that his servants whispered, David perceived that the child was dead: therefore David said unto his servants, Is the child dead? And they said, He is dead. (20) Then David arose from the earth, and washed, and anointed himself, and changed his apparel, and came into the house of the LORD, and worshipped: then he came to his own house; and when he required, they set bread before him, and he did eat. *(2 Samuel 12:16-20)*

Ten-day fast: Daniel observed a ten-day Partial Fast from the king's meat. They only ate pulse and water: "Prove thy servants, I beseech thee, ten days; and let them give us pulse to eat, and water to drink" *(Daniel 1:12)*.

We see a fourteen-day fast when Paul was on the ship bound for destruction: "And while the day was coming on, Paul besought them all to take meat, saying, This day is the fourteenth day that ye have tarried and continued fasting, having taken nothing" *(Acts 27:33)*.

Twenty-one day fast: "(2) In those days I Daniel was mourning three full weeks. (3) I ate no pleasant bread, neither came flesh nor wine in my mouth, neither did I anoint myself at all, till three whole weeks were fulfilled" *(Daniel 10:2, 3)*.

Forty-day fast: Moses observed two forty-day fasts with no drink or food: "Thus I fell down before the LORD forty days and forty nights, as I fell down at the first; because the LORD had said he would destroy you" *(Deuteronomy 9:25)*. Elijah went forty days in the strength of the food provided by God: "And he arose, and did eat and drink, and went in the strength of that meat forty days and forty nights unto Horeb the mount of God" *(1 Kings 19:8)*. Jesus fasted forty days: "(1) Then was Jesus led up of the Spirit into the wilderness to be tempted of the devil. (2) And when he had fasted forty days and forty nights, he was afterward an hungred" *(Matthew 4:1, 2)*. Moses is the only man in the Bible that did two forty-day fasts; Jesus and Elijah did one.

Allow the LORD to help you choose your fast through the Scriptures. He knows your abilities and disabilities. His main purpose for you to fast is to empty yourself of your own strength and rely fully on His.

I have had the privilege to meet many wonderful men of God, many of them youth pastors. One in particular gave me his testimony that will help you understand the need to allow God to tell you how long to fast:

The Power and Importance of Fasting

As a Youth Pastor, it is my heart's desire to see teenagers come to a saving knowledge of Christ but not to stop there! I long to see teens come to a place in their life that they have a passion to live for Christ daily! We do not run a Youth Ministry to provide a social club for teens to keep them off the streets and out of trouble. We are here to see lives changed for the Glory of God!

A few years back it seemed as though there were no teens in our youth ministry that had any concern for spiritual things. It felt like I could preach my heart out to them and love them, yet they just did not care about anything concerning God. I got so very discouraged and even seriously contemplated quitting. At one point I had even written out my resignation stating that we needed to get a youth pastor that could "reach" these teens.

God really convicted my heart in some major ways. One

way that He worked on me was in this area of fasting. God seemed to specifically tell me that if I really wanted to see these teens change, why don't I get serious about praying for that change! One thought God plagued me with was if our teens were as spiritually strong in direct relation to how much I pray for them, would there be any spiritual depth at all? With that conviction in mind, God told me to start fasting to see some changes.

I determined to fast for a day. At the end of day one, as hungry as could be, God told me to fast for day two as well. Two days turned into a week. I never dreamed I would ever or could ever fast for a week. Still I was seeing no change at all—as if to think that it would change immediately anyway! At the end of one week, as clear as could be, God was telling me to continue. Finally, at the end of forty days, God finally let me eat. I was sure that things would be different after fasting as much as I did, but I noticed no change in the teens, but I did see a great change in me! God had done a great work in me! I was experiencing a Heaven-sent revival! As I changed, I then started to see our teens change. God started a revival in our youth ministry that spread throughout our entire church. Even today, we still are experiencing the blessings of what God did as a direct result of someone getting serious about getting ahold of God! Fasting truly does make a difference!

This is a wonderful testimony for a number of reasons. First, the question "How serious are you?" is in the formula for his fast. Next, it backs up the fact that God will direct you in the amount of time you should fast. It also shows that even though God did not answer his prayer the way he chose, He did give him rejuvenation in his own life and ministry. Again, you are not going to back God into a corner and force Him to answer your prayer the way you desire, but you are giving God the liberty to move in your life the way He pleases. It is a much better plan to have God in full control of your life! The last thing we see is, the end results came a short while after his fast was ended. God did the work in his life and then later gave him the results for which he fasted. We serve a wonderful God who will give you the desires of your heart.

"Now, therefore, in compliance with the request, and fully concurring in the views of the Senate, I do, by this my proclamation, designate and set apart Thursday, the 30th. day of April, 1863, as a day of national humiliation, fasting and prayer. And I do hereby request all the People to abstain, on that day, from their ordinary secular pursuits, and to unite, at their several places of public worship and their respective homes, in keeping the day holy to the LORD, and devoted to the humble discharge of the religious duties proper to that solemn occasion."

ABRAHAM LINCOLN

— CHAPTER SIX —

THE PROCLAIMED
Fast

When the leader of a nation knows the power of God and has a holy reverence for Him, he will implement proclaimed days of fasting and prayer. The very foundation of our country was based on this practice. On March 2, 1863, Senator James Harlan of Iowa introduced a resolution in the Senate to ask President Lincoln to implement a national day of prayer and fasting. This resolution was accepted and signed into law by President Lincoln on March 30, 1863.

> Now, therefore, in compliance with the request, and fully concurring in the views of the Senate, I do, by this my proclamation, designate and set apart Thursday, the 30th day of April, 1863, as a day of national humiliation, fasting and prayer. [29]

It is a great privilege to live in a country that has allowed God to have a part in its existence. What a sad report that the leaders the people of America have recently voted into office obviously do not understand the necessity of allowing the God of Heaven to have His place in our nation. On April 15, 2010, U.S. District Judge Barbara Crabb made this ruling in a federal court hearing:

> It goes beyond mere 'acknowledgment' of religion because its sole purpose is to encourage all citizens to engage in prayer, an inherently religious exercise that serves no secular function in this context, she wrote. In this instance, the government has taken sides on a matter that must be left to individual conscience.[30]

Although the religious freedom America has enjoyed is under heavy attack from the forces of evil, our nation will continue to recognize the National Day of Prayer. This is a portion of the letter recorded from the White House under President Obama's leadership after Judge Crabb made her ruling:

NOW, THEREFORE, I, BARACK OBAMA, President of the United States of America, do hereby proclaim May 7, 2009, as a National Day of Prayer. I call upon Americans to pray in thanksgiving for our freedoms and blessings and to ask for God's continued guidance, grace, and protection for this land that we love.[31]

Some fasts were proclaimed in the Bible for the entire Israelite nation to observe for specific and religious reasons.

(27) Also on the tenth day of this seventh month there shall be a day of atonement: it shall be an holy convocation unto you; and ye shall afflict your souls, and offer an offering made by fire unto the LORD. (28) And ye shall do no work in that same day: for it is a day of atonement, to make an atonement for you before the LORD your God. *(Leviticus 23:27, 28)*

This fast is to be kept on Yom Kippur, otherwise known as the Day of Atonement. The afflicting of the soul was to bring it into subjection. There was also the requirement of abstaining from any form of work.

King Saul proclaimed a fast during a time of battle.

And the men of Israel were distressed that day: for Saul had adjured the people, saying, Cursed be the man that eateth any food until evening, that I may be avenged on mine enemies. So none of the people tasted any food. *(1 Samuel 14:24)*

King Jehoshaphat was fearful of Moab and proclaimed a fast to seek the face of God for help.

(3) And Jehoshaphat feared, and set himself to seek the LORD, and proclaimed a fast throughout all Judah. (4) And Judah gathered themselves together, to ask help of the LORD: even out of all the cities of Judah they came to seek the LORD. *(2 Chronicles 20:3, 4)*

We can easily see the king's faith in God in verse 9: "If, when evil cometh upon us, as the sword, judgment, or pestilence, or famine, we stand before this house, and in thy presence, (for thy name is in this house,) and cry unto thee in our affliction, then thou wilt hear and help"

(2 Chronicles 20:9). Then thou wilt hear and help! Praise the LORD for such a great example of faith exercised by this Biblical character. He continued in verse 15 with these words: "…Be not afraid nor dismayed by reason of this great multitude; for the battle is not yours, but God's." God took care of the enemy and gave them a great spoil as a reward for the great faith and the obedience to seek His face through prayer and fasting!

Joel received instruction from God to declare a fast among the people:

> (12) Therefore also now, saith the LORD, turn ye even to me with all your heart, and with fasting, and with weeping, and with mourning: (13) And rend your heart, and not your garments, and turn unto the LORD your God: for he is gracious and merciful, slow to anger, and of great kindness, and repenteth him of the evil. (14) Who knoweth if he will return and repent, and leave a blessing behind him; even a meat offering and a drink offering unto the LORD your God? (15) Blow the trumpet in Zion, sanctify a fast, call a solemn assembly: *(Joel 2:12-15)*

Great and precious are His promises! "And it shall come to pass, that whosoever shall call on the name of the LORD shall be delivered:" *(Joel 2:32)*.

The king of Nineveh proclaimed a fast when he heard of the coming destruction of his city. Jonah had come to the city to preach the coming destruction because of the people's wickedness. Upon hearing the truth of sure destruction, the king proclaimed a fast and put the lives of his people into the hands of our merciful God: "So the people of Nineveh believed God, and proclaimed a fast, and put on sackcloth, from the greatest of them even to the least of them" *(Jonah 3:5)*. We know that the nation of Nineveh was spared from the wrath of God due to the fasting and prayers of the people.

A fast was proclaimed during the reign of King Jehoiakim: "And it came to pass in the fifth year of Jehoiakim the son of Josiah king of Judah, in the ninth month, that they proclaimed a fast before the LORD to all the people in Jerusalem, and to all the people that came from the cities of Judah unto Jerusalem" *(Jeremiah 36:9)*.

Ezra proclaimed a fast to seek the LORD for the will of God in their lives and the lives of the children: "Then I proclaimed a fast there, at the river of Ahava, that we might afflict ourselves before our God, to seek of him a right way for us, and for our little ones, and for all our substance" *(Ezra 8:21)*.

We have seen how Queen Esther proclaimed a fast to save the nation from the evil man Haman.

> Go, gather together all the Jews that are present in Shushan, and fast ye for me, and neither eat nor drink three days, night or day: I also and my maidens will fast likewise; and so will I go in unto the king, which is not according to the law: and if I perish, I perish. *(Esther 4:16)*

After the great victory the Jews had experienced, the sons of Haman were dead, and the Jews were free from danger for the time being, feasting and rest were in order: "But the Jews that were at Shushan assembled together on the thirteenth day thereof, and on the fourteenth thereof; and on the fifteenth day of the same they rested, and made it a day of feasting and gladness" *(Esther 9:18)*. There is a time to rest, eat, and be refreshed.

> (18) Behold that which I have seen: it is good and comely for one to eat and to drink, and to enjoy the good of all his labour that he taketh under the sun all the days of his life, which God giveth him: for it is his portion. (19) Every man also to whom God hath given riches and wealth, and hath given him power to eat thereof, and to take his portion, and to rejoice in his labour; this is the gift of God. (20) For he shall not much remember the days of his life; because God answereth him in the joy of his heart. *(Ecclesiastes 5:18-20)*

Mordecai and Esther proclaimed a fast as a time of remembrance for this great deliverance. According to the *Jewish Virtual Library*, the fast of Esther is still observed today.

> On the 13th of Adar, the Fast of Esther is observed in memory of the Fast observed by Mordechai and Esther and all Israel. On that very day, the enemies of the Jews had planned to subjugate and destroy them. The opposite, however, occurred and the Jews ruled over their enemies. The practice of fasting was observed by the people of Israel whenever they were faced by war. Thus Moshe Rabenu also fasted when he came to wage war against Amalek. The aim of the fast was to affirm that a man does not prevail by physical or military strength, but only by lifting his eyes heavenward in prayer so that Divine Mercy might give him the strength to prevail in battle. This then was the purpose

of the fast observed by Israel at the time of Haman, when they gathered to defend themselves against those who sought to destroy them. And in memory of that Fast, a yearly Fast was fixed for generations on the same day. We are to recall thereby that God accepts each person's prayer and penitence in the hour of his trouble.[32]

Isaiah 58 is one of the great chapters in the Bible concerning fasting. The LORD is very gracious to give us record in His Word of the rewards and benefits we can obtain from a life of fasting.

(8) Then shall thy light break forth as the morning, and thine health shall spring forth speedily: and thy righteousness shall go before thee; the glory of the LORD shall be thy rereward. (9) Then shalt thou call, and the LORD shall answer; thou shalt cry, and he shall say, Here I am. If thou take away from the midst of thee the yoke, the putting forth of the finger, and speaking vanity; (10) And if thou draw out thy soul to the hungry, and satisfy the afflicted soul; then shall thy light rise in obscurity, and thy darkness be as the noonday: (11) And the LORD shall guide thee continually, and satisfy thy soul in drought, and make fat thy bones: and thou shalt be like a watered garden, and like a spring of water, whose waters fail not. (12) And they that shall be of thee shall build the old waste places: thou shalt raise up the foundations of many generations; and thou shalt be called, The repairer of the breach, The restorer of paths to dwell in. *(Isaiah 58:8-12)*

The statement was made to me by Dr. Charles Keen that "fasting people must be creative people." As I have studied this great topic and have implemented the principles in my life, I can understand what he meant. People that believe in the old-fashioned way of reaching the throne of grace with our requests can expect great things from our God: "But without faith it is impossible to please him: for he that cometh to God must believe that he is, and that he is a rewarder of them that diligently seek him" *(Hebrews 11:6)*.

"A true leader that loves his people will be willing to humble himself through fasting on behalf of his flock."

CHAPTER SEVEN

REASONS
to Fast

There are many different reasons to fast recorded in our Bible. These are examples given to us as guidelines for why, when, and how to fast. Each individual today can find reasons to add fasting to his prayer life. Below, you will find some of the examples that are listed for us in God's Word for our instruction.

Abraham's eldest servant was given the task of finding a wife for Isaac. Not just any wife would do; Abraham wanted one that came from his kindred, a wife that would share his beliefs and customs. The eldest servant was a very loyal man and did not want to disappoint Abraham. By faithfully serving Abraham for many years, he must have witnessed how Abraham had received favor from God when he found himself in a difficult situation that demanded divine intervention. He wanted assurance that God had heard and answered his prayer according to Abraham's request: "And there was set meat before him to eat: but he said, I will not eat, until I have told mine errand..." *(Genesis 24:33)*. The servant had set his guidelines for his fast and was determined to stay within those guidelines. God honored his fast and gave him assurance that Rebekah was the one.

Moses, the man of God, was meeting with the LORD concerning instruction for God's chosen people. "And he was there with the LORD forty days and forty nights; he did neither eat bread, nor drink water. And he wrote upon the tables the words of the covenant, the ten commandments" *(Exodus 34:28)*. Moses was the leader of the people and placed himself directly in the will of God for their benefit. He was also willing to stand before God, on the people's behalf, begging God to change His mind about destroying them:

(10) Now therefore let me alone, that my wrath may wax hot against them, and that I may consume them: and I will make of thee a great nation. (11) And Moses besought the LORD his God, and said, LORD, why doth thy wrath wax hot against thy people, which thou hast brought forth out of the land of

Egypt with great power, and with a mighty hand. *(Exodus 32:10, 11)*

A true leader that loves his people will be willing to humble himself through fasting on behalf of his flock.

The fast on the Day of Atonement was designed for a day of rest from our physical labor, but also a day to receive rest for our souls:

> (29) And this shall be a statute for ever unto you: that in the seventh month, on the tenth day of the month, ye shall afflict your souls, and do no work at all, whether it be one of your own country, or a stranger that sojourneth among you: (30) For on that day shall the priest make an atonement for you, to cleanse you, that ye may be clean from all your sins before the LORD. (31) It shall be a sabbath of rest unto you, and ye shall afflict your souls, by a statute for ever. *(Leviticus 16:29-31)*

This rest can only come when we are convicted of our sin and repent, asking the LORD for forgiveness. A life of self-denial will assure us that God is faithful to forgive us and cleanse us. Resting from physical labor is a must. Our bodies need the proper amount of rest. It is also a healthy practice to allow your digestive organs to rest. This was an Old Testament ordinance, but the principle of keeping a short account with God will give us rest in our souls. Sin always causes grief.

A man or woman who was willing to separate himself unto the LORD took the Nazarite vow: "All the days of his separation he is holy unto the LORD" *(Numbers 6:8)*. This vow was a Partial Fast that was a testimony of their commitment to God. As born-again Christians, we should be willing to separate ourselves from the worldly ways that may be questionable in the eyes of God. Even if these ways may not be a direct sin against God, they could put a stumbling block in the way of an immature Christian or cause a lost sinner to have no desire to become a Christian. We are ambassadors of another country and need to let the world know there is something different about us. The appearance and the abstinence from worldly ways put a badge of Godliness on the person who was under the Nazarite vow.

Moses went before God the second time begging God not to destroy the people. This is without a doubt a Supernatural Fast. Moses went for a total of eighty days without food or water while receiving the Ten Commandments:

(18) And I fell down before the LORD, as at the first, forty days and forty nights: I did neither eat bread, nor drink water, because of all your sins which ye sinned, in doing wickedly in the sight of the LORD, to provoke him to anger. (19) For I was afraid of the anger and hot displeasure, wherewith the LORD was wroth against you to destroy you. But the LORD hearkened unto me at that time also. *(Deuteronomy 9:18, 19)*

Very few men are willing to suffer the afflictions of fasting on behalf of the people they lead. Moses was a living example of how a leader of God's people should be willing to deny himself through fasting so the flock can receive benefits from God. God will do supernatural things in our lives, too! "The world has yet to see what God can do with and for and through and in and by the man who is fully and wholly consecrated to Him. I will try my utmost to be that man." (D.L. Moody)[33] Oh, for men and women who would have such a desire!

The children of Israel were fasting to receive counsel from the LORD. This was a time of war, and the people were seeking guidance from God concerning the battle: "Then all the children of Israel, and all the people, went up, and came unto the house of God, and wept, and sat there before the LORD, and fasted that day until even, and offered burnt offerings and peace offerings before the LORD" *(Judges 20:26)*.

Hannah fasted, begging God to open her womb: "(6) And her adversary also provoked her sore, for to make her fret, because the LORD had shut up her womb. (7) And as he did so year by year, when she went up to the house of the LORD, so she provoked her; therefore she wept, and did not eat" *(1 Samuel 1:6, 7)*.

As Samuel spoke to all the house of Israel, they fell into deep conviction. They drew water and poured it out, signifying the pouring out of their hearts before the LORD in regret and repentance for their sin. They also added fasting to show the LORD they were truly sorrowful about their denial of the true and living God. They were preparing to serve the LORD with all of their hearts, hoping that God would spare them from the hand of the Philistines: "And they gathered together to Mizpeh, and drew water, and poured it out before the LORD, and fasted on that day, and said there, We have sinned against the LORD. And Samuel judged the children of Israel in Mizpeh" *(1 Samuel 7:6)*.

Jonathan was angry for the dreadful way his father had treated David and the fact that his father also hurled a javelin at him in a fit of rage. He fasted because of his anger and grief for the outrageous treatment his father had exhibited toward his friend David: "So Jonathan arose from the table in fierce anger, and did eat no meat the second day of the month: for he was grieved for David, because his father had done him shame" *(1 Samuel 20:34)*.

Saul's appetite was taken away due to his fear of God's judgment: "Then Saul fell straightway all along on the earth, and was sore afraid, because of the words of Samuel: and there was no strength in him; for he had eaten no bread all the day, nor all the night" *(1 Samuel 28:20)*.

The "valiant men" fasted for seven days while mourning the death of Saul and his sons:

> (11) And when the inhabitants of Jabeshgilead heard of that which the Philistines had done to Saul; (12) All the valiant men arose, and went all night, and took the body of Saul and the bodies of his sons from the wall of Bethshan, and came to Jabesh, and burnt them there. (13) And they took their bones, and buried them under a tree at Jabesh, and fasted seven days. *(1 Samuel 31:13)*

David and all the men that were with him fasted when hearing the horrible news of the death of Saul and Jonathan: "(11) Then David took hold on his clothes, and rent them; and likewise all the men that were with him: (12) And they mourned, and wept, and fasted until even, for Saul, and for Jonathan his son, and for the people of the LORD, and for the house of Israel; because they were fallen by the sword" *(2 Samuel 1:11, 12)*.

It was David's custom to fast when he was mourning the loss of a friend. Here we see him fasting for the loss of Abner: "And when all the people came to cause David to eat meat while it was yet day, David sware, saying, So do God to me, and more also, if I taste bread, or ought else, till the sun be down" *(2 Samuel 3:35)*. Notice how his example pleased the people: "And all the people took notice of it, and it pleased them: as whatsoever the king did pleased all the people" *(2 Samuel 3:36)*.

Uriah fasted from marital relations with his wife while the rest of his comrades were still in the battle: "And Uriah said unto David, The ark, and Israel, and Judah, abide in tents; and my LORD Joab, and the servants of my LORD, are encamped in the open fields; shall I then go into mine house, to eat and to drink, and to lie with my wife? as thou livest, and as thy soul liveth, I will not do this thing" *(2 Samuel 11:11)*. He was more concerned for his fellow soldiers than he was satisfying his flesh. This is a great example of self-discipline and concern for his fellow soldiers during the time of war.

David fasted for the health of his child. He knew he was under God's chastening hand and was serious about doing what he could to change the mind of God. This account in the Bible has given comfort to the multitudes of people who have had to bury a child:

> (16) David therefore besought God for the child; and David fasted, and went in, and lay all night upon the earth. (17) And the elders of his house arose, and went to him, to raise him up from the earth: but he would not, neither did he eat bread with them. (18) And it came to pass on the seventh day, that the child died. And the servants of David feared to tell him that the child was dead: for they said, Behold, while the child was yet alive, we spake unto him, and he would not hearken unto our voice: how will he then vex himself, if we tell him that the child is dead? (19) But when David saw that his servants whispered, David perceived that the child was dead: therefore David said unto his servants, Is the child dead? And they said, He is dead. (20) Then David arose from the earth, and washed, and anointed himself, and changed his apparel, and came into the house of the LORD, and worshipped: then he came to his own house; and when he required, they set bread before him, and he did eat. (21) Then said his servants unto him, What thing is this that thou hast done? thou didst fast and weep for the child, while it was alive; but when the child was dead, thou didst rise and eat bread. (22) And he said, While the child was yet alive, I fasted and wept: for I said, Who can tell whether God will be gracious to me, that the child may live? (23) But now he is dead, wherefore should I fast? can I bring him back again? I shall go to him, but he shall not return to me. *(2 Samuel 12:16-23)*

In 1 Kings 13:8-24, we see a prophet that was given a mission and a direct charge from God not to eat or drink: "(8) And the man of God said unto the king, If thou wilt give me half thine house, I will not go in with thee, neither will I eat bread nor drink water in this place: (9) For so was it charged me by the word of the LORD, saying, Eat no bread, nor drink water, nor turn again by the same way that thou camest" *(I Kings 13:8, 9)*.

He was obedient to a call of God for his mission but allowed another prophet to convince him it was okay to eat and drink because he, too, had heard from God. This old prophet lied but was convincing enough to cause the younger prophet to disobey and ultimately suffer punishment for his disobedience:

And when the prophet that brought him back from the way heard thereof, he said, It is the man of God, who was disobedient unto the word of the LORD: therefore the LORD hath delivered him unto the lion, which hath torn him, and slain him, according to the word of the LORD, which he spake unto him. *(I Kings 13:26)*

Pride has a way of causing men, even good men, to stray from the oracles of God. What else could have been the reason for the old prophet to lie, other than jealousy? The man of God should take heed here not to compare one man's work to another's or allow the sin of jealousy of another man's ministry to cause him to speak contrary to the Word of God. The old prophet's life was spared, but no doubt his offense against the young prophet haunted him for the rest of his life.

After Ahab heard from Elijah about God's judgment on his wicked deeds, he fasted and begged God for mercy:

(27) And it came to pass, when Ahab heard those words, that he rent his clothes, and put sackcloth upon his flesh, and fasted, and lay in sackcloth, and went softly. (28) And the word of the LORD came to Elijah the Tishbite, saying, (29) Seest thou how Ahab humbleth himself before me? because he humbleth himself before me, I will not bring the evil in his days: but in his son's days will I bring the evil upon his house. *(1 Kings 21:27-29)*

Elijah had found Ahab and proclaimed God's judgment on him. After hearing the sentence passed for his wickedness, King Ahab humbled himself before God and found mercy. As our merciful God has promised to any who will repent, Ahab found forgiveness. This act of humility only postponed the passing of judgment from his lifetime to his children's.

Saul's valiant men fasted for his death and burial: "They arose, all the valiant men, and took away the body of Saul, and the bodies of his sons, and brought them to Jabesh, and buried their bones under the oak in Jabesh, and fasted seven days" *(1 Chronicles 10:12).*

Because of fear due to the approaching enemy, Jehoshaphat went before the LORD with great earnest. He called for a corporate fast when he heard that the adversary was upon them:

(1) It came to pass after this also, that the children of Moab, and the children of Ammon, and with them other beside the Ammonites, came against Jehoshaphat to battle. (2)

Then there came some that told Jehoshaphat, saying, There cometh a great multitude against thee from beyond the sea on this side Syria; and, behold, they be in Hazazontamar, which is Engedi. (3) And Jehoshaphat feared, and set himself to seek the LORD, and proclaimed a fast throughout all Judah. (4) And Judah gathered themselves together, to ask help of the LORD: even out of all the cities of Judah they came to seek the LORD. *(2 Chronicles 20:1-4)*

As the leader of the people, Jehoshaphat wanted direct intervention from God to help in the battle. He was not only concerned for his own life, but also for the people God had given him to lead. The corporate fast, called by a leader, is one that brings men together to show God their trust in Him and to seek His hand in the conflict. There is always power in numbers. There have been many fasts proclaimed by Christian leaders during the presidential elections in America. Knowing that a wicked president will lead a country contrary to God's Word, fasting and praying could determine the destiny of an entire nation, as it did in Jehoshaphat's instance. What joy must have overcome his heart when he heard the answer from the LORD: "And he said, Hearken ye, all Judah, and ye inhabitants of Jerusalem, and thou king Jehoshaphat, Thus saith the LORD unto you, Be not afraid nor dismayed by reason of this great multitude; for the battle is not yours, but God's" *(2 Chronicles 20:15)*.

Ezra proclaimed a fast while seeking the right way for the people and the children: "Then I proclaimed a fast there, at the river of Ahava, that we might afflict ourselves before our God, to seek of him a right way for us, and for our little ones, and for all our substance" *(Ezra 8:21)*. As a spiritual leader, he knew that the people needed to learn the importance of seeking the direction of God in the midst of a battle through fasting. He was familiar with the practice and the power it produced. He also had a great concern for the future leaders of the nation. It is so important that the younger generation see how serious the current Christian leaders are about seeking God. Note the product that a season of fasting produced: "Then we departed from the river of Ahava on the twelfth day of the first month, to go unto Jerusalem: and the hand of our God was upon us, and he delivered us from the hand of the enemy, and of such as lay in wait by the way" *(Ezra 8:31)*.

Ezra mourned over the sins of those exiled: "Then Ezra rose up from before the house of God, and went into the chamber of Johanan the son of Eliashib: and when he came thither, he did eat no bread, nor drink water: for he mourned because of the transgression of them that had been carried away" *(Ezra 10:6)*. Many times mourning a loss will cause you to lose your appetite. In this case, it is quite possible that Ezra was so overwhelmed with grief that he had no desire to eat. We also see Nehemiah fasting when he heard of the condition of his fellow Jews in Nehemiah 1:1-4.

The children of Israel gathered in a corporate fast over the sins and iniquities of the nation: "Now in the twenty and fourth day of this month the children of Israel were assembled with fasting, and with sackclothes, and earth upon them" *(Nehemiah 9:1)*. America could see a great revival if the Christians of this once great nation would corporately fast and pray for God's mighty power to send it.

Some of the Jews were fasting due to the judgment passed on the entire race: "And in every province, whithersoever the king's commandment and his decree came, there was great mourning among the Jews, and fasting, and weeping, and wailing; and many lay in sackcloth and ashes" *(Esther 4:3)*.

Esther called for a corporate fast as she accepted the challenge to go before the king to have the decree changed: "Go, gather together all the Jews that are present in Shushan, and fast ye for me, and neither eat nor drink three days, night or day: I also and my maidens will fast likewise; and so will I go in unto the king, which is not according to the law: and if I perish, I perish" *(Esther 4:16)*.

Great physical pain led to Job's lack of nourishment: "(19) He is chastened also with pain upon his bed, and the multitude of his bones with strong pain: (20) So that his life abhorreth bread, and his soul dainty meat" *(Job 33:19, 20)*.

David fasted for his enemies when they were sick: "But as for me, when they were sick, my clothing was sackcloth: I humbled my soul with fasting; and my prayer returned into mine own bosom" *(Psalm 35:13)*. This is a Biblical principle taught by Christ in the New Testament: "But I say unto you, Love your enemies, bless them that curse you, do good to them that hate you, and pray for them which despitefully use you, and persecute you" *(Matthew 5:44)*.

Depression caused the psalmist to not eat: "My heart is smitten, and withered like grass; so that I forget to eat my bread" *(Psalm 102:4)*.

Hunger and thirst were the result of rebellion to God's way:

(1) O give thanks unto the LORD, for he is good: for his mercy endureth for ever. (2) Let the redeemed of the LORD say so, whom he hath redeemed from the hand of the enemy; (3) And gathered them out of the lands, from the east, and from the west, from the north, and from the south. (4) They wandered in the wilderness in a solitary way; they found no city to dwell in. (5) Hungry and thirsty, their soul fainted in

them. (6) Then they cried unto the LORD in their trouble, and he delivered them out of their distresses. *(Psalm 107:1-6)*

God's Word records for us that many lose their desire to eat and will suffer with serious illness as a result of their mutiny to God's mode of living: "Their soul abhorreth all manner of meat; and they draw near unto the gates of death" *(Psalm 107:19)*.

Isaiah 58 is the chapter where we see God's chosen fast for the Jews and the results of it: "Is not this the fast that I have chosen? to loose the bands of wickedness, to undo the heavy burdens, and to let the oppressed go free, and that ye break every yoke" *(Isaiah 58:6)*.

Daniel, Hananiah, Mishael, and Azariah fasted from food that had been offered to false gods. They asked their captors if they could be exempt from the king's meat and remain on the Jewish diet: "Prove thy servants, I beseech thee, ten days; and let them give us pulse to eat, and water to drink" *(Daniel 1:12)*. God honored their fast with strength and wisdom, which led to their promotion while in captivity. God will honor a Christian who abstains from the worldly ways in the secular world. We are to be in the world but not of the world.

King Darius fasted for Daniel while he was in the den of lions: "Then the king went to his palace, and passed the night fasting: neither were instruments of musick brought before him: and his sleep went from him" *(Daniel 6:18)*.

Daniel fasted and prayed as he confessed the sins of the people: "And I set my face unto the LORD God, to seek by prayer and supplications, with fasting, and sackcloth, and ashes" *(Daniel 9:3)*.

Daniel was in mourning because of the condition of his people. It was for this purpose he set his face to seek and understand God. Please note in verse 12 how God heard his prayer: "Then said he unto me, Fear not, Daniel: for from the first day that thou didst set thine heart to understand, and to chasten thyself before thy God, thy words were heard, and I am come for thy words" *(Daniel 10:12)*.

The sorrow and shame of the people led to a day of fasting and prayer. They knew the judgment of God was at hand: "(14) Sanctify ye a fast, call a solemn assembly, gather the elders and all the inhabitants of the land into the house of the LORD your God, and cry unto the LORD, (15) Alas for the day! for the day of the LORD is at hand, and as a destruction from the Almighty shall it come" *(Joel 1:14, 15)*.

God commands the people to turn to Him with all their hearts (repentance), to weep, and to fast: "Therefore also now, saith the LORD, turn ye even to me with all your heart, and with fasting, and with weeping, and with mourning" *(Joel 2:12)*.

The king proclaimed a fast because of a repentant heart. The fast was to beg God for mercy and to plead with Him to change His mind about destroying the city: "And he caused it to be proclaimed and published through Nineveh by the decree of the king and his nobles, saying, Let neither man nor beast, herd nor flock, taste any thing: let them not feed, nor drink water" *(Jonah 3:7)*.

The fast found in Zechariah's time was to express joy, gladness, cheerfulness, and the love of truth and peace. It was part of religious practices: "Thus saith the LORD of hosts; The fast of the fourth month, and the fast of the fifth, and the fast of the seventh, and the fast of the tenth, shall be to the house of Judah joy and gladness, and cheerful feasts; therefore love the truth and peace" *(Zechariah 8:19)*.

Jesus fasted forty days and forty nights in preparation for His ministry: "And when he had fasted forty days and forty nights, he was afterward an hungred" *(Matthew 4:2, Luke 4:2)*.

Extraordinary manifestation of the hand of God can only come through prayer and fasting: "Howbeit this kind goeth not out but by prayer and fasting" *(Matthew 17:21)*.

Jesus fasted from sleep while praying: "Watch ye and pray, lest ye enter into temptation. The spirit truly is ready, but the flesh is weak" *(Mark 14:38)*.

Anna served God with fasting: "And she was a widow of about fourscore and four years, which departed not from the temple, but served God with fastings and prayers night and day" *(Luke 2:37)*.

The Pharisee fasted as part of his list of good deeds hoping that they would someday take him to Heaven: "I fast twice in the week, I give tithes of all that I possess" *(Luke 18:12)*. From this passage, we see religious practices that cause afflictions, even those conducted in the deepest sincerity, are done in vain if exercised as a means to redeem people from their sin.

Jesus did not eat because He was busy with His Father's work: "Jesus saith unto them, My meat is to do the will of him that sent me, and to finish his work" *(John 4:34)*.

Saul was seeking guidance after his conversion: "And he was three days without sight, and neither did eat nor drink" *(Acts 9:9)*.

Cornelius, a Gentile, was fasting because he feared God and wanted his people to know the truth: "And Cornelius said, Four days ago I was fasting until this hour; and at the ninth hour I prayed in my house, and, behold, a man stood before me in bright clothing" *(Acts 10:30)*.

Paul and Barnabas fasted as they prepared to leave on their mission: "As they ministered to the LORD, and fasted, the Holy Ghost said, Separate me Barnabas and Saul for the work whereunto I have called them" *(Acts 13:2)*.

Paul and Barnabas fasted when ordaining the elders of the new churches: "And when they had ordained them elders in every church, and had prayed with fasting, they commended them to the LORD, on whom they believed" *(Acts 14:23).*

Even sinners fast and take vows to receive favor from their gods: "And when it was day, certain of the Jews banded together, and bound themselves under a curse, saying that they would neither eat nor drink till they had killed Paul" *(Acts 23:12).*

The men in the boat were fasting because it looked like sure doom for them: "And while the day was coming on, Paul besought them all to take meat, saying, This day is the fourteenth day that ye have tarried and continued fasting, having taken nothing" *(Acts 27:33).* When trouble arises in a huge way, even unbelievers will call out to God for help.

It is a good practice to abstain from certain food that could cause the weaker brother to stumble: "It is good neither to eat flesh, nor to drink wine, nor any thing whereby thy brother stumbleth, or is offended, or is made weak" *(Romans 14:21, 1 Corinthians 8:13).*

Fasting from marital relations for a season is a weapon to keep the devil from tempting you with perverted sexual thoughts and actions. Satan will tempt with lack of self-control over sexual desires: "Defraud ye not one the other, except it be with consent for a time, that ye may give yourselves to fasting and prayer; and come together again, that Satan tempt you not for your incontinency" *(1 Corinthians 7:5).*

Fasting was included in the list of elements the Apostle Paul noted for approving yourself as a minister of God. When you are an effective minister or a servant of God, it will include fasting: "(4) But in all things approving ourselves as the ministers of God, in much patience, in afflictions, in necessities, in distresses, (5) In stripes, in imprisonments, in tumults, in labours, in watchings, in fastings" *(2 Corinthians 6:4, 5).*

The Apostle Paul includes fasting in the perils of the preacher: "In weariness and painfulness, in watchings often, in hunger and thirst, in fastings often, in cold and nakedness" *(2 Corinthians 11:27).*

In the latter days, religious practices will include abstaining from meat and marriage: "Forbidding to marry, and commanding to abstain from meats, which God hath created to be received with thanksgiving of them which believe and know the truth" *(1Timothy 4:3).* This is a very common practice among different religions today.

As you can see, there are many different reasons for fasting recorded in the Bible. Our lives are no different than those who have gone before us. Christians suffer with lost loved ones, children out of the will of God, children on the battlefield, sickness, etc. By adding fasting to our prayers, we will have peace in the answer with which God chooses to respond.

Fasting will also prepare us for the work God has called us to do. "Howbeit this kind goeth not out but by prayer and fasting" *(Matthew 17:21)*. Christ did not insinuate that the disciples had to go on a fast to handle a particular situation, but He was telling the men that they needed to develop a life of fasting to seek the ultimate power available through fasting coupled with prayer.

It was during a revival meeting at the Hillsboro West Regional Detention Center in Tampa, Florida, when this valuable lesson became evident. As the Rock of Ages team entered the detention center, an awful howling noise echoed off the concrete walls. As we made our way down the hall to the first unit, I looked into a lock-down cell that contained an eleven-year-old boy yelling at the top of his lungs, pulling on his head, running into the walls and jumping around like a wild man; he had no desire to talk to the preacher. The team went into the unit across the hall to conduct our service. I began to talk to the LORD about this young man, pleading with Him to allow me the chance to talk to this boy. In my prayer, I told the LORD how members of the Juvenile Team had not only prayed for young people like this, but we had fasted on a regular basis for His power over demons.

As the team left the first unit on the way to the next, the boy had calmed down and was gazing out the six-by-twelve window of the lock down cell. I walked over to him and could see he was now ready to listen. I took him to Mark chapter 5 and showed him the Biblical account of how Jesus took a crazy man and put him back in his right mind. I asked him if he had ever heard how Jesus turned a maniac into a missionary? His reply was a shake of the head as if to say, "No." I showed him how Jesus was able to make the devils leave the crazy man and to give him his right mind back. When I was finished with the Gospel presentation, this young boy bowed his head and trusted the LORD Jesus Christ as his personal Saviour.

There was another boy in the cell next to his that had been kicking his door. When I approached the cell door, I could see he, too, was very troubled. He allowed me to share the Gospel with him using the very same text as I did with the previous boy. This young man also trusted the LORD. His trouble stemmed from facing five years in an adult facility. This young man was seventeen years old and would serve the next five years of his life in an adult prison, but he would not have to face it alone. The One who saved the maniac of Gadara lives inside him and will lead and guide him. All praise, honor, and glory go to our wonderful LORD and Saviour!

When dealing with the juveniles of America, you will definitely face demonic activity. We are in a spiritual warfare, and the devil will do all he can to destroy the life of a teenager.

During a revival in a children's home, God dealt with a disturbed young lady, leading us to have a very eventful night. She threw herself to the ground and began bashing her head into the floor. Some of the congregation sang about the blood while others read verses about Christ and His precious blood! I held her head to keep it from hitting the floor while three other men held her legs and arms. After a season of prayer, she calmed down long enough to call on Christ for help and for salvation. I do not know how many; but through the power of the blessed Holy Ghost, a bunch of demons found themselves homeless that night. God said to my heart, *You and the team were ready for this battle through prayer and fasting!*

Fasting is a form of worship and communication with the LORD separate from prayer. In no way are you to try to force God to answer your prayer according to your will, but fasting will demonstrate to Him your willingness to afflict yourself, or humble yourself, in order for God to show you His will in your need. It gives the LORD a sense of urgency in your request and shows Him your total confidence in the teachings of His precious Word, the KING JAMES BIBLE. It displays to Him how serious you are! If you are serious about reaching souls for Christ, living a life of power, and giving God the green light to do a great work in your life and ministry, add fasting to your prayers. Again, you cannot manipulate God by your fast. You must pray in His will not yours.

Fasting can bring revival to you, your family, and a nation: "If my people, which are called by my name, shall humble themselves, and pray, and seek my face, and turn from their wicked ways; then will I hear from heaven, and will forgive their sin, and will heal their land" *(2 Chronicles 7:14)*.

What a comfort it is to know that God has given us (Christians) His name! Those who have called upon the LORD Jesus Christ, repenting or turning from their sins, believing that He was born of a virgin, lived thirty-three and a half years on the earth, was tempted in all points yet knew no sin, died on the cross of Calvary, was buried, rose the third day—praise God!—and is sitting at the right hand of the Father, are given God's name. If you are born again, trusting in Jesus and Him alone, you are His child: "But as many as received him, to them gave he power to become the sons of God, even to them that believe on his name" *(John 1:12)*. Now that we have established, to whom God is talking, let's see what he commands.

The very first thing He tells us we must do is to humble ourselves. This word humble has the meaning of placing yourself under subjection. "Humble yourselves therefore under the mighty hand of God, that he may exalt you in due time" *(1 Peter 5:6)*. The LORD has pleasure in the exaltation of His saints. When we humble ourselves, it is as if to say to the LORD we trust Him to give us the strength to be used by Him. Fasting from food or some form of pleasure is a way of our giving ourselves to God. We rely on Him for strength, both physically and mentally, to endure the period in which we are afflicting our bodies for His cause. In this humbling process, we are totally depriving ourselves of the pleasure of physical nutrition in order to receive spiritual nourishment.

When Christians grow to such a level of maturity that they trust God with every area of their lives, the promise of power is the result. "(5) Trust in the LORD with all thine heart; and lean not unto thine own understanding. (6) In all thy ways acknowledge him, and he shall direct thy paths" *(Proverbs 3:5, 6)*. We, as men, want to take charge; but the man who humbles himself before God will accomplish much more than one who goes in his own power.

Until we realize that power comes from God, we will never have His power to accomplish great things for Him: "God hath spoken once; twice have I heard this; that power belongeth unto God" *(Psalm 62:11)*. So many times we try to operate in our own power. We fail to remember that all we are and all of our accomplishments are because He has allowed us to be used. When we humble ourselves before God, He then can use us as a mere channel of His power and love.

We must be careful not to fall into the trap of being proud that we are being used. It is a daily battle to fight against all of the fiery darts of the wicked: "Above all, taking the shield of faith, wherewith ye shall be able to quench all the fiery darts of the wicked" *(Ephesians 6:16)*. Pride is the number one dart that is hurled by the devil. No doubt, pride was the destruction of Saul, David, Solomon, Samson, and many other Biblical characters.

During this time of humbling or fasting, prayer plays a very important part. If the LORD so chooses during your season of prayer and fasting, you may be ushered into the presence of the Holy God where you can experience the closeness to Him you desire. Please do not try to manipulate God! You are sadly mistaken if you think that fasting will cause God to do what you want, the way you want it, and when you want it. God knows what is best in every situation in life and will do what He chooses knowing it is the best for you: "And we know that all things work together for good to them that love God, to them who are the called according to his purpose" *(Romans 8:28)*. If you are seeking closeness to the LORD, you are promised to find Him: "...The LORD is with you, while ye be with him; and if ye seek him, he will be found of you; but if ye forsake him, he will forsake you" *(2 Chronicles 15:2).* David forsook God for a brief time, and the chastening hand of the Almighty God delivered the blows that would haunt him for the rest of his life.

Just when you think it will not happen to you, the devil and all of Hell will unleash temptation after temptation to try to bring you down. Remember to pray for our fallen brethren: "Wherefore let him that thinketh he standeth take heed lest he fall" *(1 Corinthians 10:12).*

The seeking of God's face is not the same as God's hand. When you are seeking His face, you are seeking to be in His presence. When ushered into His presence, you are able to accomplish great things for Him and through Him. It is in His presence where you will desire to please Him: "Therefore came I forth to meet thee, diligently to seek thy face, and I have found thee" *(Proverbs 7:15).*

God has given us direction on how to come into His presence: "Let us come before his presence with thanksgiving, and make a joyful noise unto him with psalms" *(Psalm 95:2).* The first recorded requirement to come into His presence is to come with thanksgiving. The word *thanksgiving* has the implication of adoring Him. It is like a choir of worshipers singing at the top of their lungs praise to His Name. It also can be thought of as a time of confessing His marvelous works and confessing our insufficiency to work on our own.

We are to come into His presence adoring Him and praising Him with a psalm on our heart. According to Noah Webster's 1828 Dictionary the word *adoration* means:

> 1. The act of paying honors to a divine being; the worship paid to God; the act of addressing as a God....Adoration consists in external homage, accompanied with the highest reverence. It is used for the act of praying, or preferring requests or thanksgiving, to the Supreme Being........

> 2. Homage paid to one in high esteem; profound reverence.......Adoration, among the Jews, as performed by bowing, kneeling and prostration. Among the Romans, the devotee, with his head uncovered, applied his right hand to his lips, bowing and turning himself from left to right. The Persians fell on the face, striking the forehead against the earth, and kissing the ground. The adoration paid to the Grecian and Roman emperors, consisted in bowing and kneeling at the feet of the prince, laying hold of his robe, then withdrawing the hand and clapping it to the lips. In modern times, adoration is paid to the pope by kissing his feet, and to princes, by kneeling and kissing the hand. This word

was used by the Romans for acclamation or great applause, given to public performer; and the election of a pope is sometimes by adoration, that is, by sudden acclamation without scrutiny.

We are to come confessing our sins and praising Him for allowing us the privilege to be in His presence. We are to come in an attitude of worship with a song on our hearts.

He commands us to turn from our wicked ways. If you are not willing to forsake the sin in your life, there is no sense in fasting: "He that covereth his sins shall not prosper: but whoso confesseth and forsaketh them shall have mercy" (Proverbs 28:13). "If I regard iniquity in my heart, the LORD will not hear me" (Psalm 66:18). Someone once said that sin will take you farther than you want to go, keep you longer than you want to stay, and cost you more than you want to pay. If holding on to iniquity means unanswered prayer, your sin is very costly!

God demands repentance in order to have fellowship: "Testifying both to the Jews, and also to the Greeks, repentance toward God, and faith toward our LORD Jesus Christ" (Acts 20:21). Dr. Ron Gearis, former president of Rock of Ages Prison Ministry, says this about repentance:

> Siamese twins. By the way, they each have a name. One is named repentance and the other one is named faith. Repentance is born first. Always, in your Bible, when the two things are named, repentance is first. And faith follows because they are Siamese twins."[34]

It is impossible to have the saving faith if you do not have a repentant heart. You cannot have one without the other.

In the same God Save America Conference, Dr. Jon Jenkins said this in his message entitled, What a God:

> My Friend, belief is the part of the Gospel that our motivation is centered upon. We want to get to Heaven, which is why we get saved. That is the truth. But that was not ever God's motivation for salvation. God's motivation for salvation was to get His young ones back. And, friend, the reason you believe is so that you can go to Heaven. But the reason you need to repent is so that God can get His young one back.[35]

When we put our faith in Christ, we receive salvation. That is our part. When we repent, then God gets His child back. That is God's part. If there is no change, there was no salvation: "God shall hear, and afflict them, even he that abideth of old. Selah. Because they have no changes, therefore they fear not God" *(Psalm 55:19)*. The fear of God is the beginning of wisdom. How can one be saved if there is no desire to change in his heart? God gives the repentance to those who desire to have it; this is the repentance that saves.

> (8) If we say that we have no sin, we deceive ourselves, and the truth is not in us. (9) If we confess our sins, he is faithful and just to forgive us our sins, and to cleanse us from all unrighteousness. (10) If we say that we have not sinned, we make him a liar, and his word is not in us. *(1 John 1:8-10)*

The repentance God is referring to in this verse is His children in a backslidden condition. Christians in this condition need to turn from their sinful ways, confess them, and restore the relationship with the Father.

After these requirements are accomplished in our meeting with the LORD, He then promises to heal our land. God always keeps His end of the deal! You can rest assured that revival can and will come to your life, your family's lives, your children's lives and our great country, if Christians would be satisfied with a fasting and prayer ministry. You may never be a great preacher in the public eye, and you may never stand before thousands of people to preach the Gospel, but wherever you are, you could accomplish as much as a preacher would by having a ministry of prayer and fasting before our LORD.

Set a time aside where you and God meet every day. He will help you as you seek Him in the area of fasting. You can set aside a specific time to fast. Your health may not permit you to fast from food for a long period of time. You can commit to the LORD to skip a meal on a regular basis. The great Fulton Street Revival of years past started when Jeremiah Lanphier committed to fast and pray for revival in America during his lunch hour every day. He hung a sign on the church door and said he was praying for America during his lunch hour and if you would like to join him you could. The church building soon was full, the prayer meetings spread on to other churches in the area, and soon a great revival swept across America: "Again I say unto you, That if two of you shall agree on earth as touching any thing that they shall ask, it shall be done for them of my Father which is in heaven" *(Matthew 18:19)*.

Was the great revival due to the preaching? Although the preaching of God's Word played a very significant role, I believe it was the answer to the fasting and prayers of many ordinary servants of God: "And he said unto them, This kind can come forth by nothing, but by prayer and fasting" *(Mark 9:29).*

Fasting can break the power of sin over your flesh. One man was molested at age nine, and the abuse continued for some years. This abuse led him to believe he was a homosexual. In his heart he knew that lifestyle was wicked and tried desperately to have victory over it. He even got married to camouflage his homosexuality. After hearing a message preached about the power of fasting, he began an extended fast to beg God for victory over the demonic oppression involved in this wicked sin. He made a list of the requests with which he desired to have God help him. He wanted to be totally free from homosexual thoughts, pornography, masturbation, and a gossiping tongue. He also wanted to restore his love with his wife, become a prayer warrior, obtain a spirit of humility, have financial freedom, and be able to recognize that Christ was active in his life. This man was asking God for a miracle. According to his own testimony, halfway through the fast he became very hungry. It did not seem as if God was helping him with his homosexual thoughts. He almost quit but decided to ask God for renewed strength. He said that it was then when the LORD showed him that he was under demonic oppression. The last day of his fast he realized that he had been set free from the bondage of the demonic stronghold of homosexuality. He felt totally delivered, free, and clean. This man had a heart desire to be released from the sin that held him in bondage. Through fasting, God gave him the victory. God is able and wants to give you victory over your sin, also.

Fasting can also give you a hedge of protection and great results in your ministry. In the book *Power through Prayer and Fasting* by Ronnie W. Floyd,[36] the story is told of some Godly men in his church. Thirty of the men got together and committed to fast and pray one day a week for their pastor. Each man chose a different day so they were fasting and praying 24/7. These men were called "Pastor's Mighty Men." Around the clock, the pastor had someone fasting and praying that he would have the power of God on him, that he would not fall into sin, that he would stay healthy, that his marriage would remain strong, and many other things as well. The results were phenomenal.

We are given a list of precious promises and rewards to those who fast.

(8) Then shall thy light break forth as the morning, and thine health shall spring forth speedily: and thy righteousness shall go before thee; the glory of the LORD shall be thy rereward [The part of an army that marches in the rear, as the guard;

the rear guard.]. (9) Then shalt thou call, and the LORD shall answer; thou shalt cry, and he shall say, Here I am. If thou take away from the midst of thee the yoke, the putting forth of the finger, and speaking vanity; (10) And if thou draw out thy soul to the hungry, and satisfy the afflicted soul; then shall thy light rise in obscurity, and thy darkness be as the noonday: (11) And the LORD shall guide thee continually, and satisfy thy soul in drought, and make fat thy bones: and thou shalt be like a watered garden, and like a spring of water, whose waters fail not. (12) And they that shall be of thee shall build the old waste places: thou shalt raise up the foundations of many generations; and thou shalt be called, The repairer of the breach, The restorer of paths to dwell in. *(Isaiah 58:8-12)*

With so many Biblical references to fasting, one could easily see that fasting is a discipline that is pleasing to God, and it is an avenue of putting a sense of urgency to your request. When the average church member realizes that there is much more to being a Christian than a Sunday morning trip to church, we could once again see a great revival sweep across this nation. J. Harold Smith said, "We are empty of grace and full of grease."[37]

No one believes in the power of prayer and fasting like the Devil. He does not practice it, but he suffers great loss from the results of it!

— CHAPTER EIGHT —

The D R Y *Season*

Some would have the tendency to believe that through an extended period of fasting they would expect to have a remarkable experience of joy and peace. Some may even expect some kind of divine manifestation from the LORD. This can be true, if the LORD so desires; but for the most part, my personal experiences with extended fasting seem to be very dry spiritually. These dry spells can be referred to as spiritual attacks. Derek Prince warns us in his book *How to Fast Successfully* of the spiritual attacks that we may encounter during our fasts.[38]

On May 18, 2009, the thirty-second day of my water-only fast I recorded this in my journal:

> I did not even pick up my Bible today other than to read a Proverb so I could write a devotion. It is so weird! I so bad want to be directly in His presence, but the cares of the every day work are really getting to me. I mowed today, and I had to do it in shifts. I am so very weak, and my throat is so dry. I still have so much mucus draining down the back of my throat; it is very uncomfortable. I sent my devotion out late this evening. Brother Mark Brown sent this note back to me: "Brother Mike, I read this verse and thought of you tonight. I love this, 'Then said he unto me, Fear not, Daniel: for from the first day that thou didst set thine heart to understand, and to chasten thyself before thy God, thy words were heard, and I am come for thy words' *(Daniel 10:12)*. God has been listening, my Brother; your words have been heard. Your Brother, Mark."
>
> I wept as I read this note and just cried unto the LORD to show me His glory. I so desperately need to go to the wilderness! I need to just go tomorrow and spend some time in the woods. With His help, I will do this!

For some reason, after day thirty-two I did not make any more journal entries. I do know this for sure: it was the very next day, day thirty-three, that I made my way to a friend's house who allowed me to use his four-wheeler. I rode through the woods to a pavilion, way up on a hill, and began to pray and read my New Testament. While I was in the wilderness both physically and spiritually, God came to meet with me! As I read, the LORD directed me to this wonderful verse: "But watch thou in all things, endure afflictions, do the work of an evangelist, make full proof of thy ministry" *(2 Timothy 4:5).* God gave me the peace and settled in my heart His calling into the international work.

I looked up the definition of the number *three* in the book *Numbers in the Bible* by Robert D. Johnston and found this definition:

There are in measurement three dimensions, length, breadth, and thickness. These go to make up solid, and therefore speaks of solidity. It is the symbol of completeness. This solidity and completeness suggests the Triune God, hence three denoted Divine testimony or manifestation. This manifestation, or Divine perfection, is also the symbol of resurrection. Next to seven, it is the most commonly used number in the Bible.[39]

I find it no coincidence that God showed me my verse on the thirty-third day of my fast. It is a solid fact in my heart that God has called me to travel the world as long as He will physically and financially allow me!

My dry spell, although very difficult to endure, seemed to come to an end that day in the woods. The next seven days would continue to be very dry due to my physical condition, but the peace of knowing God's perfect will for our future gave me the necessary strength to finish.

It could just be a compliment that God would allow you to endure a season of harassment from the devil! We do know that Job's dry spell was approved from Headquarters. It just may be the devil is at the Throne of God asking permission to try to discourage you during your fast when God says, "Have you considered my servant?" What an honor to have the stinking old devil attack while we are in direct obedience to God in seeking Him through prayer and fasting. We must not get discouraged; God is on our side: "But I am poor and needy; yet the LORD thinketh upon me: thou art my help and my deliverer; make no tarrying, O my God" *(Psalm 40:17).*

It is faith that pleases God in today's economy, a faith that does not demand a miraculous event that would move you to follow Jesus with all of your heart. We have been given a Bible and the blessed Holy Ghost as our guide. It is of great necessity that we trust that God is real and that He still uses the same avenues to obtain His power as He did during the writing of His Word. God moved upon holy men to write the Bible, and He moves on holy men to follow it as well. Jesus rebuked the Pharisees when they asked Him for some miraculous sign:

> (11) And the Pharisees came forth, and began to question with him, seeking of him a sign from heaven, tempting him. (12) And he sighed deeply in his spirit, and saith, Why doth this generation seek after a sign? verily I say unto you, There shall no sign be given unto this generation. (13) And he left them, and entering into the ship again departed to the other side. *(Mark 8:11-13)*

Notice that after Jesus had rebuked them for seeking a sign, He left them. Dry spells are mostly self-inflicted. It is best to remain satisfied that one day we will live in His presence eternally! We must daily seek to serve Him, worship Him, and adore Him. We must remember continuously what Christ told Thomas, "Jesus saith unto him, Thomas, because thou hast seen me, thou hast believed: blessed are they that have not seen, and yet have believed" *(John 20:29)*.

The dry season can be a true compliment when you simply believe even though you have not seen. The book, *Experiencing the Depths of Jesus Christ*, by Jeanne Guyon, has been referred to as "one of the most helpful and powerful Christian books ever written."[40] In her book she makes this statement:

> The LORD Jesus is looking about everywhere for that Christian who will remain faithful and loving even when He has withdrawn Himself. If the LORD finds such a faithful soul, when He does return, He rewards the faithfulness of His child. He pours out upon that faithful one abundant goodness and tender caresses of love.[41]

"Hogs and humans are the only creatures on earth that keep their stomachs loaded twenty-four hours a day."

DR. J. HAROLD SMITH

— CHAPTER NINE —

FASTING
is Healthy

"Fasting is the oldest, most effective healing method known to man."[42] Think back on the young man in the juvenile prison who said he was going to fast from cussing. Fasting from a sin seems quite funny; when you begin to think about the fact that we are killing ourselves with the food we eat, we, too, should fast from this sin. Evangelist Billy Kelly was reported to have said that he killed himself with a fork and a spoon. This evangelist had the power of God on his ministry, yet because of his weakness in the area of food, his work was cut short. According to Wikipedia, the online encyclopedia:

> Obesity is a leading preventable cause of death worldwide, with increasing prevalence in adults and children, and authorities view it as one of the most serious public health problems of the 21st century. Obesity is stigmatized in much of the modern world (particularly in the Western world), though it was widely perceived as a symbol of wealth and fertility at other times in history, and still is in some parts of the world.[43]

"Preventable" is the word that seems to stand out in the above statement. Some physical ailments are not preventable, but one can gain control over what and how much he puts into his mouth. God has given each of us our bodies and has allowed us to be stewards over them. He refers to our bodies as His temple: "(19) What? know ye not that your body is the temple of the Holy Ghost which is in you, which ye have of God, and ye are not your own? (20) For ye are bought with a price: therefore glorify God in your body, and in your spirit, which are God's" *(1 Corinthians 6:19, 20)*. Just like God has trusted us with the tithe, which belongs to Him, He has also trusted us to maintain our bodies physically for Him. Once you have been purchased, you no longer are your own; this includes your body as well as spirit and soul. Since we are worth His precious blood as a purchase price, we should be careful to do our best to keep our bodies in good shape for His glory. We are to keep our bodies in good health because He has also trusted us with the greatest story that has ever been told: "But as we were allowed of God to be put in trust with the gospel, even so we speak; not as pleasing men, but God, which trieth our hearts" (I Thessalonians 2:4). How can we spread the Good News if we have destroyed our bodies with a fork and a spoon?

Further research in Wikipedia on the health benefits from fasting has given a light on the physical profits of fasting:

> Glucose is the body's primary fuel source and is essential for the brain's functioning. When denied glucose for more than 4–8 hours, the body turns to the liver for glycogen, a storage form of glucose, to be used for fuel. A process called glycogenolysis converts glycogen into a usable form of fuel. At this point, the body also uses small amounts of protein to supplement this fuel. This fuel will last for up to 12 hours before the body needs to turn to glycogen stored in muscles, lasting for a few more days. If glucose is still denied at this point, muscle wasting is prevented by temporarily switching to fat as the fuel source, with glucose made as a byproduct during ketosis. The brain can then use this glucose or even ketones as a fuel source, while the rest of the body thrives on primarily fat. The body continues to use fat for as long as there is fat to consume. The body will generally indicate to the faster when fat levels are running extremely low (less than 7% and 10% of body weight for males and females, respectively) with an increased urge for food. Fasts are usually broken long before this point. If the fast is not broken, starvation begins to occur, as the body begins to use protein for fuel. Health complications associated with fast-induced starvation include electrolyte imbalances, thinning hair, lanugo, cardiac arrhythmia and renal failure. Death can occur if fasting is pursued to the point of complete starvation.

> Research suggests there are major health benefits to caloric restriction. Benefits include reduced risks of cancer, cardiovascular diseases, diabetes, insulin resistance, immune disorders, and more generally, the slowing of the aging process, and the potential to increase maximum life span. According to Dr. Mark P. Mattson, chief of the laboratory of neurosciences at the US National Institute on Aging, fasting every other day (intermittent fasting) shows

beneficial effects in mice as strong as those of caloric-restriction diets, and a small study conducted on humans at the University of Illinois indicates the same results. According to the US National Academy of Sciences, other health benefits include stress resistance, increased insulin sensitivity, reduced morbidity, and increased life span. Long-term studies in humans have not been conducted. However, short-term human trials showed benefits in weight loss. The side effect was that the participants felt cranky during the three week trial. According to the study conducted by Dr. Eric Ravussin, "Alternate-day fasting may be an alternative to prolonged diet restriction for increasing the life span."

Adherence to Greek Orthodox fasting periods contributes to an improvement in the blood lipid profile, including a decrease in total and LDL cholesterol, and a decrease in the LDL to HDL cholesterol ratio. A statistically insignificant reduction in HDL cholesterol was also observed. These results suggest a possible positive impact on the obesity levels of individuals who adhere to these fasting periods.

Changes in blood chemistry during fasting, in combination with certain medications, may have dangerous effects, such as increased chance of acetaminophen poisoning. Excessive fasting for calorie restrictive purposes, accompanied by intense fears of becoming overweight are associated with mental disturbances, including anorexia nervosa.[44]

Studies have shown that most health problems can be traced back to eating habits. In today's drive-thru society, fat and cholesterol are the number one items on the menu. It is so easy to just grab a burger and fries, wash it down with a Coke, all to camouflage the hunger instead of maintaining your body's health. As the years go by, the results of these unhealthy eating habits will mean frequent trips to the doctor, disease, with the end result summed up in this statement, "Out of service!"

Looking into the Greek Orthodox practice of fasting, I found some interesting statements:

Gluttony makes a man gloomy and fearful, but fasting makes him joyful and courageous. And, as gluttony calls forth greater and greater gluttony, so fasting stimulates greater and greater endurance. When a man realizes the grace that comes through fasting, he desires to fast more and more. And the graces that come through fasting are countless.... Saint Nikolai of Zicha.[45]

The Orthodox church has a calendar for regular fasting days. They believe that fasting is a very essential part of life for both physical and spiritual aspects:

Fasting is an *essential* aspect of practicing the Orthodox life. You cannot be Orthodox and not fast. Unfortunately, many in the Church today do not participate in this grace-bestowing and life-giving ascetic practice. They do this to the loss of their own spiritual and bodily health.[46]

I am not a Greek Orthodox; I am a Baptist and proud of it. Fasting is practiced by many religions to obtain favor with God. I am glad that I do not have to practice fasting to go to Heaven, but that does not mean it does not have its benefits. Whether you go by the Greek Orthodox outline for fasting or the Dr. Bragg's way of fasting, you can rest assured there are many physical rewards for your discipline. In the book *Celebration of Discipline*, Richard J. Foster says this concerning the discipline of fasting: "Our freedom in the gospel, however, does not mean license; it means opportunity. Since there are no laws that bind us, we are free to fast on any day. Freedom for the apostle Paul meant that he was engaged in "fastings often" *(2 Corinthians 11:27, KJV)*."[47] We are reminded in the Bible not to abuse our liberties: "For, brethren, ye have been called unto liberty; only use not liberty for an occasion to the flesh, but by love serve one another" *(Galatians 5:13)*. Fasting for the right reasons and doing it the right way will produce the right results.

Dr. Herbert M. Shelton is probably the greatest expert on the topic of fasting known to man. He personally supervised over 40,000 fasts.[48] In 1978, he helped found the International Association of Professional Natural Hygienists (IAPNH). This organization has set the standards and practices for conducting therapeutic fasts.[49] In his book *Fasting Can Save Your Life*; he makes this observation concerning the topic of fasting:

Few subjects going back in mankind's history are so widely misunderstood, in our modern, high-caloric civilization, as fasting. The important role it can play, and has played, is often distorted in the public mind, or twisted out of shape by grotesque and groundless fears, based not on truth but on prejudiced, scientific misinformation or complete lack of information.[50]

Dr. Shelton gives a wonderful story of a seventy-year-old man who had very bad asthma attacks for many years. [51] Along with his asthma, he also had a deaf ear, an enlarged prostate, and sinus troubles, and other medical ailments. He had been through all the standard treatments for his asthma and was on all of the pharmaceutical aids money could buy. Tired of standard treatments with no results, he checked himself into an institution that would put him on a supervised fast. The first thing they did was remove all of his medication from him and put him in a place where he could relax. He was a bit nervous about having an attack but was assured that he could grit his teeth and endure it. The story ends with amazing results. After forty-two days of water only, one miracle after another occurred. He no longer had asthma, his sinuses were clear as ever, and his hearing even came back to his left ear. Dr. Shelton states that his case was not unusual with the exception of the variety of conditions that were cured. [52]

Fasting Can Save Your Life is a book that you must read if you are serious about your health! Dr. Shelton says that "fasting is the most natural and the most sensible means of care of the body of which we have any knowledge." [53]

Chapter 2 of his book is titled "Pounds That Slip Away." Dr. Shelton says this about fasting for weight loss:

> Not only is there safety in fasting for weight reduction, there is also greater ease than there is in dieting. One reason for this is that unlike almost all dieters, the faster is not hungry all the time. His taste buds are not always tempting him. The flood of gastric juices is not being constantly activated. [54]

J. Harold Smith said: "Hogs and humans are the only creatures on earth that keep their stomachs loaded twenty-four hours a day." [55]

Remember, each individual experience is unique. I personally have experienced hunger most of the time during my fasts. All of my fasting, up to this date, have been for spiritual reasons rather than health. It could be that the spiritual fast is more demanding physically due to the spiritual battle. Many times Satan will tempt you to break your commitment and end the fast before the set time. He knows that God will honor the fast that is completed, and, for this reason, he will do anything he can to get you to eat. It is very important when you make a commitment to God to fast for a particular amount of time that you keep your vow: "Better is it that thou shouldest not vow, than that thou shouldest vow and not pay" *(Ecclesiastes 5:5)*. Remember, God gave Satan full control of Job's health with the exception of taking his life.

> (4) And Satan answered the LORD, and said, Skin for skin, yea, all that a man hath will he give for his life. (5) But put forth thine hand now, and touch his bone and his flesh, and he will curse thee to thy face. (6) And the LORD said unto Satan, Behold, he is in thine hand; but save his life. (7) So went Satan forth from the presence of the LORD, and smote Job with sore boils from the sole of his foot unto his crown. *(Job 2:4-7)*

Dr. Shelton continues to say,

> I state these facts out of my own personal experiences but they are also verified by investigations. Two series of experiments carried out by regular medical men in accredited hospitals, have developed empirical evidence sufficient to satisfy the experimenter scientifically that fasting is not only a safe and speedy way of reducing weight, but is also the most comfortable way of reducing.[56]

The two experiments he is speaking of were conducted in the Piedmont Hospital in Atlanta, Georgia, by Lyon Bloom, M.D. and by Garfield Duncan, M.D., of the University of Pennsylvania. Dr. Duncan has been considered an authority on weight reduction.[57]

Next to Dr. Herbert M. Shelton, two of the greatest experts on the health benefits from fasting are Paul Bragg and his daughter, Patricia Bragg. Their book *The Miracle of Fasting*[58] gives all the benefits one could ever imagine from practicing fasting. I highly recommend that you get a copy of their book and examine for yourself all the physical benefits from fasting. Patricia says, "Fasting is not starving, it's natures cure that God has given us."[59] God has given us other avenues of healing than the pharmacy! Patricia Bragg says, "Fasting is the best detoxifying method. It's also the most effective and safest way to increase elimination of waste buildups and enhance the body's miraculous self-healing and self-repairing process that keeps you healthy and youthful."[60] She goes on to say,

> Fasting works by self-digestion. During a fast your body

intuitively will decompose and burn only the substances and tissues that are damaged, diseased or unneeded, such as abscesses, tumors, excess fat deposits, excess water and congestive wastes. Even a short fast (1-3 days) will accelerate elimination from your liver, kidneys, lungs, bloodstream and skin.[61]

Life and death are in the hands of God. "Bragg (Paul) suffered an accident in 1976 at the age of 81. He was injured by a wave in the surf in Hawaii. His health started to decline, and six months later he died of a heart attack in Miami, Florida." [62] Lester Roloff practiced healthy eating and died in a plane crash. This does not give us the right to abuse our bodies rendering them useless before their time. If we will do our best to maintain a healthy diet and exercise regularly, we can have a much easier life. In his book, Bragg tells us:

Flesh is dumb! It has no intelligence or reasoning power. If, after reading this book, you are convinced, without any reservations, that a fasting program is going to elevate you to greater heights of living, then your mind becomes the master of your flesh! Your mind must be stronger than the desires of your flesh, because your body has long been conditioned to have food put into it at various intervals of the day. [63]

The Apostle Paul admonishes us in 2 Corinthians 10 concerning our flesh:

(3) For though we walk in the flesh, we do not war after the flesh: (4) (For the weapons of our warfare are not carnal, but mighty through God to the pulling down of strong holds;) (5) Casting down imaginations, and every high thing that exalteth itself against the knowledge of God, and bringing into captivity every thought to the obedience of Christ; (6) And having in a readiness to revenge all disobedience, when your obedience is fulfilled. *(2 Corinthians 10:3-6)*

Improper eating habits can be overcome by allowing God to help. If you seek Him in a season of fasting, He will help you overcome this deadly lifestyle. One preacher who had severe blood sugar problems said this, "If it tastes good, spit it out!" It made us all laugh, but the truth is, it does not have to come in a wrapper to taste good. There are many different foods and recipes that are not only tasty but also healthy. These can be easily accessed on the Internet.

We are God's instruments to carry His message to a lost and dying world. He needs an army of healthy, vibrant, and alert soldiers. Taking care of our bodies is as important as our ministries. If we cannot physically accomplish the task God has called us to do because of the way we have treated our bodies, shame on us!

Dr. Bragg says that he believes that the average person can fast for ten days without any complications. He states that, "The 10 day fast results in a great amount of internal housecleaning." [64] Bragg recommends a twenty-four to thirty-six hour fast weekly. He also says that four times a year you should fast seven to ten days. [65]

Dr. Bragg gives us a list of powerful affirmation to go by during our fast. First, he says, "I have this day to put my body in the hands of God...I turn to the highest power for internal purification and rejuvenation of body and soul." Second, "Every minute that I fast I am flushing dangerous poisons that do great damage from my wonderful body. Every hour that I fast I become happier, healthier and have more energy and youthfulness." Third, "Hour by hour, my body is cleansing and purifying itself." Fourth, "When I fast I am using the same method for physical, mental and spiritual purification that the greatest spiritual leaders have used throughout the ages." Last, "I am in complete control of my body during this fast. No false hunger pains will stop me from fasting! I will carry my fast through to a successful conclusion because I have total faith in God." [66]

One of the greatest rewards of fasting in the physical realm is renewed energy. Anytime excess weight is lost, the energy level will increase. We live in a world of "energy in a can" that usually produces an extreme amount of energy for a short time and then the crash! Most of these energy drinks are loaded with caffeine, which will cause more damage than good. At the conclusion of your fast, you will have a noticeable amount of energy until you begin to bog down your system with the same old eating habits.

There are many more physical benefits that can be attributed to fasting. I also recommend Dr. Bragg's book if you are seriously seeking a life of fasting for health reasons. Some may think that fasting is a cure for disease, but Bragg is very clear when he says, "Fasting is not a cure for any disease or ailment. The purpose of a fast is to allow the body's Vital Force full range and scope to fulfill its own self-healing, self-repairing and self-rejuvenating functions to the best advantage." [67]

Again, I am not a medical doctor! For this reason, none of this information is to be considered medical counsel. Please consult a physician who is aware of the physical benefits attributed to fasting.

In the preface to the second edition of Dr. Shelton's book *Fasting Can Save Your Life*, he gives us warnings about what medical doctors and other health books are saying about fasting.[68] Fasting is not starvation! Starvation means that you are dying because of lack of the essential elements needed to survive. Dr. Shelton says, "Fasting is a biological process and belongs to the world of life."[69] There are many withdrawal symptoms one will endure during his fast. When your body is used to having tea, coffee, soft drinks, and candy bars on a regular basis, it will have adverse reactions to abstaining from them for a season. Some may refer to these as "side effects," but, in essence, they are withdrawal symptoms from the poison these items contain. You can have dizziness, headaches, weakness, trembling, and pains in the abdomen, back, and joints. It is possible that you may vomit, become very nauseated, and even faint. It is not recommended to drink coffee, tea, soft drinks, strained soups, or broth during your fast. It is best to stay with purified water only. To maintain a healthy lifestyle, it is best to leave these unhealthy elements out of your diet permanently. They are killing you before your time!

When you begin an extended fast, you can expect certain physical developments. Your tongue will have a heavy white coating on it, and, pardon the expression, but your breath will stop a freight train. Your teeth may become pasty, and you will have a bad taste in your mouth. This process is really a cleansing process. You are eliminating dangerous toxins that have built up in your body. As your fast takes care of the toxins, your tongue will return to a normal color, and your mouth and breath will be clean and sweet.[70]

You will probably suffer from severe headaches. Some may call them a "hungry headache," but really it is probably a withdrawal symptom from the effects of heavy doses of caffeine. Your urine will go through a series of changes, too. It may be light to begin with but will eventually get dark and have a very foul odor. It is possible that it could even turn black.[71] It is also possible that vomiting may occur during extended fasting. If it persists, it may be a sign of dehydration; at this time, you should consider breaking your fast. [72]

After much study on the health benefits of fasting, it can be said that fasting for health reasons has meaningful benefits. When conducted in a supervised fashion, fasting is very rarely dangerous to your health. If you are considering an extended fast for health reasons, please get a copy of *Fasting Can Save Your Life* and *The Miracle of Fasting*. These two books are loaded with a wealth of information concerning the benefits of fasting.

"Go on a hunger strike for
the glory of God."

DR. J HAROLD SMITH

— CHAPTER TEN —

BREAKING
the Fast

The phrase "young and dumb" comes to mind when I rehearse my early days of fasting. Coming off of an extended fast requires the strictest of discipline. Your fast is now complete, and all you can think of is eating everything and anything you want. I had concluded my first fast, seventeen days, with only water. I was at the home of a supporting pastor when my fast came to an end. His wife had prepared an awesome home-cooked meal, and I was ready and eager to eat. I had chicken, potatoes and gravy, a vegetable, and, of course, a chocolate brownie desert, all washed down with sweet tea. I was stuffed to the gill! What happened next was not so comfortable. I was in great pain for the next three days! This was a great lesson from the school of hard knocks!

God's Word gives us clear instruction concerning the matter of breaking a fast. David's men had come across a young Egyptian man who was left to die in the field. He had not eaten or drunk any water for three days.

> (11) And they found an Egyptian in the field, and brought him to David, and gave him bread, and he did eat; and they made him drink water; (12) And they gave him a piece of a cake of figs, and two clusters of raisins: and when he had eaten, his spirit came again to him: for he had eaten no bread, nor drunk any water, three days and three nights. *(1 Samuel 30:11, 12)*

David's men gave him water, bread, a cake of figs, and raisins. The Bible is clear to tell us that this diet rejuvenated this young man.

It is very important not to overeat and to make sure you chew your food slowly and completely. Fresh fruits and vegetables are always the best way to come off of your fast. After the first day, you can have cooked vegetables. Some whole wheat bread is okay, too.

J. Harold Smith makes it clear about the difficulty of returning to normal eating after your fast is concluded: "If you think it was difficult to discipline yourself to get through the first few days of an extended fast, then you will also discover that the first few days of coming off a fast require similar discipline." [73] Moderation is the key to coming off any fast. Your mind will tell you that you have the green light to pig out, but you must bring that thought into captivity quickly. Smith tells us that our body did not go into hibernation during the fast, "But your bodily organs have been, in effect, sleeping. Gently and slowly you will want to call them back into activity." [74] Eating a large pepperoni pizza would be like sounding the reveille bugle in the ear of your organs! Not a good thing! It will taste great going down; however, the next few days will be nothing short of pure misery! Pay close attention to the suggestions for coming off of your fast.

There are different ideas about how to break your fast. All of them are quite similar but with some variations. One man suggests breaking an orange into small pieces and eating some every two hours; another man says to eat fresh, sweet fruits, such as cherries and grapes. Stewed prunes and some fresh or stewed vegetables are fine too. The pattern of each man's advice is to stay away from meats, processed food, and dairy products. After my first forty-day fast, I was advised to have pasta without sauce and a baked potato. This worked well for me.

The second forty-day fast was an easy transition. You will see in my journal that after thirty-eight and one-half days, I collapsed because I jumped up too quickly. It was then my daughter Jessica reminded me that I told the LORD I would go as long as I physically could. That night I drank some juice off of some oatmeal. The next day I had some broth from some cooked vegetables and drank some juice. When it was time to eat, I had a banana and some vegetables. I continued with oatmeal and fruit the first day, stewed vegetables the second, and eased back into some chicken the third. I highly recommend some broth when you are initially introducing food back into your diet.

It may take a few days after an extended fast for your bowels to begin working again. Be patient! They have been on shut down for a while, but your system will come back to life in a few days. Smith says that a hot bath is beneficial, and rest and relaxation is a must. [75] I have found that a half an ounce of Bragg's apple cider vinegar with a little bit of one hundred percent grape juice will help with your bowels. I have used this combination daily for many years now. It has helped to keep my cholesterol levels down and has helped with my digestive system as well.

Make very sure to eat in moderation. Your stomach has shrunk and is not used to the amount of food your brain is telling you to eat. This is a perfect time to rework your eating habits. Make sure to eat slower and chew your food really well before swallowing. When you eat slowly, your stomach has time to react to the amount of food in it and can send a message to your brain that you have had enough. We are primarily creatures of habit. You can train yourself to eat smaller portions if you desire to maintain the health you have achieved through your fast. This takes great discipline.

Enquiring from the experts is always the best. Dr. Arthur Wallis, author of *God's Chosen Fast*, considers Dr. Herbert Shelton as one of the greatest authorities on the subject of fasting in America. Dr. Shelton operated his own institution of health fasting for many years. He has supervised thousands of fasts ranging from a few days to ninety days. He has supervised people of all ages. He says that a normal, healthy person can be back to a regular eating schedule in one week after any fast of over twenty-one days.

Fasting for any period of time is not an easy practice. David said, "But as for me, when they were sick, my clothing was sackcloth: I humbled my soul with fasting; and my prayer returned into mine own bosom" *(Psalm 35:13)*. The word *humbled* has the meaning of afflicted. He also said, "My knees are weak through fasting; and my flesh faileth of fatness" *(Psalm 109:24)*. Christ told us that we are able to do all things through His power. He even went as far as to say, "Verily, verily, I say unto you, He that believeth on me, the works that I do shall he do also; and greater works than these shall he do; because I go unto my Father" *(John 14:12)*. We can and will do greater works than Christ did in His earthly ministry if we only believe and apply the same principles Christ did while He was here. Christ only had a physical earthly ministry for three and one-half years. The LORD has trusted us with His ministry and empowered us with His power. Fasting is worth it! He will bless us and sustain us as we seek Him through this wonderful process of fasting.

"We had thirty-three saved that night in the three appeals. I was convinced that the unusual moving of the Spirit of God was the result of his fasting and praying."

DR. TOM WALLACE

— CHAPTER ELEVEN —

TESTIMONIES
of Fasting

I have had the privilege of serving under and knowing some of the greatest men of God in the world. In this chapter, you will hear testimonies from some of them and also from some great Christian men and women of our day who have experienced wonderful results from fasting.

Dr. Ed Ballew and his wife Pauline were the founders of Rock of Ages Prison Ministry. The Rock of Ages web site, *www.roapm.com*, gives the information of the founding of the ministry:

> On January 5, 1978, the Rock of Ages Prison Ministry, Inc. was chartered. Dr. Ballew was President, his wife Pauline was Secretary/Treasurer, Pastor Sammy Allen was the Vice President, and local pastors formed the Board of Directors. Pastor Ron Gearis, his wife Judy, and their son Scott became the first missionary family with Rock of Ages.[76]

I had the privilege of talking with Dr. Ed Ballew on many occasions but never did ask him for a testimony of fasting. He would take me back to the little room where the tape ministry started and tell me, "This is where it all began." He would always pray for me before I left and would remind me that he prays regularly for the ministry. Dr. Ballew had a very successful ministry as an evangelist after he retired from Rock of Ages in 1987. Without a doubt, he and his dear wife practiced fasting on many occasions. He and Mrs. Pauline are now home with the LORD.

Dr. Ron Gearis was the president of the ministry when I was accepted as a missionary on May 22, 1999. I do not believe that I have ever personally met a man of God who walked any closer with our LORD than he did. Dr. Gearis always had something to say, and it would serve you well to pay close attention to what he was saying. His preaching had such an anointing on it that it seemed to leave a lasting impression on me every time he preached. Almost every message I have heard him preach has changed my life in one way or another.

103

I remember when I first met him at the home office. I had been called to the ministry when Wendell Rogers was giving his testimony about the work in Ohio. Wendell took Allen Combs, also called to Rock of Ages in the same meeting, and my wife and I to meet the staff at the home office in Cleveland, Tennessee. They talked with us for a while, and then Dr. Gearis asked me how long I had been doing volunteer work with the ministry. I told him that I had never been to prison for any reason, let alone to do volunteer work. He looked at me and told me to go home, volunteer for a while to see if I liked it, and come back if I did. I recall telling him that I would be glad to do that, but it did not matter if I liked it or not because God had called me to this ministry and if Dr. Gearis would let me, I was coming. That was in February of 1999; on May 22, 1999, I was accepted and sent out to raise support. I will always be grateful to Dr. Gearis for allowing an uneducated, green young man from the North to become a missionary with Rock of Ages!

I was just a good old boy from north central Ohio who had never heard any hard preaching from the South. Dr. Gearis was a very unique preacher who had many little sayings that did not seem to be very kind, but I soon found out that it was just his trademark. "Get behind my Lincoln. Backing over you would be pure pleasure," "Run into my fist going ninety miles an hour, Jack," "Look me in my God-given eyeball," and many other sayings of his did not seem to be like something a preacher should say. For this reason, I did not listen to the first preaching tape that was given to me during my first visit, but I anxiously listen to them now and will as long as I can! He is and always will be one of my spiritual heroes.

I had the awesome privilege to have him in my life for seven and one-half years. He went home to be with the LORD on September 12, 2006. His dear wife, Mrs. Judy—" Wifey" as he called her—survives him.

Dr. Gearis had a successful church and pastorate in Baldwin, Florida, when Dr. Ed Ballew began talking to him about the prison ministry. Wanting full assurance, Dr. and Mrs. Gearis fasted and prayed for Scripture to confirm the call. God gave each of them their own personal verse, which gave them peace to leave the church and begin a ministry that would have fruit that will remain.

Dr. Gearis had a very personal and close walk with the LORD and very seldom shared with anyone details of his intimate times with Him. Dr. Dunsford told me of a staff meeting when he came in with his prayer book and showed it to the men. He had been praying for the husband of a former church member for over thirty years. He told the men that today he could mark the prayer "Answered!" What a prayer life!

He would always tell us to "find a verse," a practical way to know God's will that I have personally implemented and instructed many people since he taught me. Just like he said, you will have peace about the decision you made when you can back it up with a verse: "Order my steps in thy word: and let not any iniquity have dominion over me" *(Psalm 119:133)*.

I asked Mrs. Judy to share with me a testimony about the fasting life of Brother Ron. (This is what most people called him.) Just as I suspected, he was a man of fasting. She told me that he would fast many times before his meetings and conferences. This is one of the reasons his preaching had such an anointing on it. Together they fasted for at least seven days to seek confirmation from God to leave a pastorate of ten years and begin a life of a missionary. Here is her response:

> After we were saved, Ron never made any major decisions without seeking the LORD for a verse of Scripture to confirm the decision.
>
> I had always just trusted the LORD by following what the LORD told Ron. But when I knew the LORD was leading about the prisons, I was fearful about leaving a very secure and happy place of service. Ten years of military life we had never lived in the same house more then two years - now I had been in the same place ten years and I am middle-aged!! The only thing I ever asked of Ron was that whatever we did we would stay together to do it. This would require major needs to accomplish this. The LORD gave me I Thessalonians 5:24: "The LORD has done it."
>
> Ron's concern was having fruit that remained. Pastoring you saw people saved and grow. Would this be the case with the inmate? The LORD gave him these verses on a Saturday evening as he was preparing for Sunday: II Peter 3:9; I Corinthians 15:58. He came out and told me, and I gave him my verse, and that next Sunday evening service he announced to the church he was resigning.
>
> His life verse when he was called to preach was II Corinthians 4:5, the verse they used for the ROA.

God gave them their confirmation through the Scriptures, which gave them the security and assurance that He would meet their needs and give them both fruit that would remain forever. Today, Rock of Ages Ministries has one hundred and forty missionaries serving here in America and around the world and, as of January 1, 2012, has recorded over five hundred thousand professions of faith. GLORY!

Dr. Gene Hooker was the vice president of the Rock of Ages during Dr. Gearis' presidency. He, too, was a man of prayer. When his son, Chris Hooker, was severely injured in a car accident, Brother Hooker would fast and pray on a number of occasions for him.

As a young man called to preach, Dr. Hooker sought God's will for his life in the ministry. A Baptist church in the area asked him to come and be their pastor. He had the best paying job he had ever had at the time they called him. He sought the LORD through prayer and fasting and received his answer; at age twenty-eight, he became their pastor.

In November 20, 1978, God used Psalm 126:6 to call Dr. Hooker to the Rock of Ages Prison Ministry. November 6, 1979, he went to Alto Prison in Georgia to be a chaplain. April 24, 1987, he became vice president of the ministry and served faithfully until the LORD called him to pastor in 2004. In June of 2010, the LORD directed him and his wife Bessie back to Rock of Ages Ministries.

After Dr. Gearis graduated to Glory on September 12, 2006, Dr. Terry Ellis would make a smooth transition into the presidency of the ministry. Dr. Ellis was the executive vice president under Dr. Gearis and was trained and ready to take this responsibility. God has used him greatly since he became the leader of the Rock of Ages.

I have the privilege to serve as the Foreign Field Representative for the Foreign Department. This gives me an opportunity to work directly with him on many occasions. It is evident in his walk with God that he, too, is a believer in fasting. Upon my request, he provided me with some great testimonies of God's direction due to fasting and prayer.

Dr. Ellis and Mrs. Peggy sought the LORD for His direction in their lives. God had been working on their hearts about joining the Rock of Ages for some time. It can be a very scary thing to leave a job that provided your only means of supporting your family. Wanting full assurance of God's calling, they went on a seven-day complete fast, no food or water. On the seventh day, Dr. Ellis was at a meeting where Brother Ed Ballew was preaching; the LORD confirmed in his heart in the service that he was to go with the Rock of Ages! When he got home, the LORD had dealt with Mrs. Peggy's heart that evening, too. With tears in her eyes, she met him at the door and told him that she knew they were going with the Rock of Ages Ministries. When God gives the confirmation in the hearts of both you and your spouse, it is clear what you should do.

Going seven days without food can be done fairly easily, but without food and water demanded special attention from the LORD to keep them from collapsing. Dr. Ellis continued with a regular schedule during his fast. It had to be God; he poured concrete in the hot Georgia sun during those days of fasting! Here is the testimony in his words:

> In the winter of 1985, I spent seven days on a total fast, praying for God's will and direction concerning full-time service for Christ. It was during this time that I worked as a concrete finisher, and my specific responsibility was screeding concrete once it was poured. It was toward the end of the week that God confirmed in our hearts that we were to give our lives to missionary service with the Rock of Ages. I immediately made application for missionary service and was accepted January 30, 1986. I quit my job two weeks later and went full-time in the ministry with $125.00 a month support. God has been faithful for 25 years to put food on our table, fuel in the tank, and to supply the demands and the needs of the ministry. I truly believe that all of this is in direct answer to a week of total fasting and seeking God's will.

Dr. Ellis provided another testimony of a time when his wife, Peggy, had an overwhelming burden to fast and pray for their children:

> This next example Peggy personally experienced when our children were young teenagers. They went with a supporting church to the country of Mexico to help do soul winning and work on a church facility. Unbeknownst to us, on the closing Saturday of the trip, the youth pastor decided to take the group to a waterfall that exceeded 100 feet in height. It was on this particular day that Peggy became very burdened for our children and came to me asking that we spend the day fasting and in prayer for both, Victoria and Randy. At 1:00 p.m. MST, Peggy's burden to pray for the children became overwhelming, and we both spent a considerable amount of time on our knees lifting our children before our Heavenly Father. Later that evening, we received a phone call from the youth pastor informing us of a close call with death that Victoria experienced while visiting the falls. The group had decided to hike to the top of the falls. There was a tree by the edge of the falls that Victoria leaned on to get a glance over the falls. When she leaned on it, the tree gave way, and she was teetering on the edge and about to fall to her death. However, in the providence of God, the youth

pastor was close enough to reach out and grab her just as she was about to go over. The youth leader and the entire group were severely shaken by this incident. We found out later that the incident happened at exactly 1:00 p.m. MST when Peggy was so overcome with a burden to pray for our children's safety.

This testimony truly does give us a great illustration of how the power of prayer and fasting exercised by parents can determine the destiny of their children!

Each year our ministry has a week of meetings called Refreshment Week. In these meetings, Dr. Ellis seeks the LORD for a topic we need to focus on for the year. The theme for the 2011 meeting was spiritual warfare. I was asked to give two forty-five minute messages on fasting. I was amazed at what the LORD did in this meeting. Here is the final testimony provided for this book from Dr. Ellis:

The third incident I would like to share is concerning our granddaughter, Dixie Mae Wonser. Recently, you (Brother Van Horn) taught on fasting and prayer during our Missionary Refreshment Week, and with it being one of the last two weeks our children were in the country before moving to the Philippines, Dixie Mae decided to sit in the auditorium with her grandmother during the services. Many times one wonders whether or not at the age of five and six, children are able to grasp what is being taught.

One week after the Refreshment Week the Wonser family moved to the Philippines and two days after they arrived, little Dixie, who is now six, was looking out the hotel window, looking at literally thousands of people walking by. Her heart was broken as she looked at the people in the city of Manila without Christ. She turned to Victoria, her mother, and asked, "Mom, can I fast and pray today like Bro. Van Horn taught us during the Missionary Refreshment Week?" Victoria asked her why she wanted to fast and Dixie replied, "I want to fast and pray that these people will get saved and give their life to Jesus." She fasted until the evening meal.

"And said unto him, Hearest thou what these say? And Jesus saith unto them, Yea; have ye never read, Out of the mouth of babes and sucklings thou hast perfected praise?" *(Matthew 21:16)*.

At the conclusion of the letter I received from Dr. Ellis was this paragraph:

On a side note Bro. Mike, thank you for teaching us about fasting and prayer. It is truly something that our generation knows little of. After our Missionary Refreshment Week one of our missionaries approached me and stated that during their four years of college they were never taught the importance of prayer in ministry, nor were they taught how to find God's will for their life, nothing about the leadership of the Holy Spirit, and they stated they were taught nothing about fasting. They attended one of our notable Independent Fundamental colleges. The missionary stated they were only taught how to develop messages, administrative procedures, organization, time management, and how to use modern technology and incorporate it into their ministry. Little was taught concerning how to develop a personal walk with Christ.

One of our missionary wives sent this note to me after our week of meetings:

I want to thank you again for the lessons on fasting that Michael brought to us in Chattanooga. We attend Resurrection Bay Baptist Church here in Seward, Alaska, and one of our members was having some serious medical problems, kidney failure among them. Naturally her husband asked us to pray for her as a church family. The LORD laid it on my heart to pray for her every Wednesday while refraining from food until after prayer meeting was over, which is about 9 p.m. She was gloriously healed by God, and as of about two weeks ago, she does not have to go to dialysis any more. This saves her a strenuous two-hour trip to Anchorage three times per week. I feel as if I had just dipped my toe into the pool of power that is fasting, but I'm ready to jump in when the LORD leads. Thanks again.

What a great testimony of the healing power of God as a direct result of prayer "and fasting"! I love what she had to say about dipping her toe into the pool of power that is fasting!

At the conclusion of the Refreshment Week, I challenged our missionaries to begin fasting for our ministry and our leaders. Dr. Ellis had a fasting calendar placed on our missionary web page, and men began to sign up. One year later, the report was that men and ladies of our ministry fasted for over six thousand hours! We experienced one of the greatest years of spiritual warfare of which I have ever been a part. On the other hand, we had the greatest year ever recorded in the history of Rock of Ages with fifty-four thousand one hundred and fifty souls making professions of faith! I am so glad there were men and women who were fasting and praying for the ministry!

I believe in this concept greatly! It would be wise if every Baptist church in the world could get men and ladies who would put a calendar together so that someone would be fasting and praying around the clock for his church and pastor: "Offer the sacrifices of righteousness, and put your trust in the LORD" *(Psalm 4:5)*. Yes, it is a sacrifice to fast, it is difficult and uncomfortable, but the rewards are out of this world.

Dr. Ricky Dunsford became the executive vice president serving with Dr. Ellis after the homegoing of Dr. Gearis. In May of 1991, the ministry began working in the prisons in Romania and now reaches five different continents. We are reaching the inmates in prisons in Brazil, Ghana, Zambia, Latvia, Lithuania, Romania, Philippines, Ukraine, Cambodia, Dominican Republic, Costa Rica, Togo, Hungary, Australia, New Zealand and are preparing to reach the Chinese people, too. Great men of God have all attained power, direction, and provision to do the work God has trusted them with the same way: righteous living, a prayer life coupled with fasting, and great faith! Dr. Dunsford was called to a nine-day complete fast (no food or water) to seek God for his calling to the international field. Truly a God-called and a God-preserving fast! Both of these current leaders of the Rock of Ages Ministries have experienced what I would call a Supernatural Fast.

Dr. Charles Keen, pastor emeritus of First Baptist Church of Milford, Ohio, and founder of First Bible International, once fasted for a day because the church needed seventy thousand dollars to pave the parking lot. A businessman who was not even a member of his church walked into his office the next day and said, "I hear you need money for your parking lot." He asked how much he needed and then wrote First Baptist Church of Milford, Ohio, a check for seventy thousand dollars! Dr. Keen told me, "Fasting people must be creative people!"

Dr. Tom Wallace pastored three great churches during his ministry: Baptist Bible Church of Elkton, Maryland (1954 to 1971), Beth Haven Baptist Church of Louisville, Kentucky (1971 to 1986), and Franklin Road Baptist Church of Murfreesboro, Tennessee (September 1, 1991, to January 2000). He has served as pastor emeritus of Franklin Road Baptist Church, Murfreesboro, Tennessee, from 2000 to the present.[77] Dr. Wallace sent me this testimony to share:

> Several years ago, I had J. Harold Smith in meetings in our church. When I picked him up at the airport on Saturday, I suggested we might get a bite to eat. He declined the

invitation and asked to be taken to his hotel room. The next day he excused himself again from the meal and shared with me that he was fasting. On Thursday he told me he was ready to eat and eat he did. He did not eat from Saturday morning until Thursday noon.

During the time there with me, he shared with me that he had on three different occasions fasted for forty days and nights. His skin was like a baby's skin. At one invitation after his sermon "God's Three Deadlines," we had around twenty respond for salvation. He came back to the pulpit before I dismissed the service two different times and continued the invitation, saying that the LORD had impressed him that others were there who needed and wanted to be saved. We had thirty-three saved that night in the three appeals. I was convinced that the unusual moving of the Spirit of God was the result of his fasting and praying.

There is no doubt that fasting will be a major component in God's Approval on your ministry:

We then, as workers together with him, beseech you also that ye receive not the grace of God in vain. (For he saith, I have heard thee in a time accepted, and in the day of salvation have I succoured thee: behold, now is the accepted time; behold, now is the day of salvation.) Giving no offence in any thing, that the ministry be not blamed: But in all things approving ourselves as the ministers of God, in much patience, in afflictions, in necessities, in distresses, In stripes, in imprisonments, in tumults, in labours, in watchings, in fastings. *(2 Corinthians 6:1-5)*

"How serious are you? Will you fast?"

— CHAPTER TWELVE —

TRIED *and* PROVEN

My first experience with fasting started early in my ministry with a morning devotion while in Tampa, Florida. I do not remember what I was reading; but in two completely different places, I came across the topic of fasting. This was back when the Rock of Ages Prison Prevention was in serious danger of discontinuing. Dr. Benny Hatfield was very sick, and Dr. Jeff King had resigned. These were the only two men working actively in the development of the public school ministry. The devil attacked the juvenile work right from the beginning and still is doing all he can to hinder the work! He will continue to fight any ministry that has a burden to see the youth reached for Christ.

We had just concluded a revival in a couple of juvenile detention centers in Tampa, Florida. My heart was heavy because of the wrecked lives of the youth in the centers. Our public school ministry was in danger of extinction; and I knew if there was hope for the youth of America, we had to keep it alive. I had a burning desire to keep Prison Prevention alive, but there was a problem. The computer technician, Brother Bill Marks, at my home church, Mansfield Baptist Temple, Mansfield, Ohio, told me that if I was going to reach this generation of students I would have to do it with high technology. He said I would need a laptop computer and a power point projector. That equipment would be no big deal today, but in the year 2000, the estimated cost was five thousand dollars. I had only been in the ministry a year or so at the time and was still working on raising my support; five thousand dollars seemed like five million to me.

I was driving home in my old Chevy Caprice after the revival meetings were finished in Florida. I became overwhelmed with the burden to keep the Prison Prevention alive in the schools. I remember weeping going down the road asking God what to do. The next thing I know, this fancy sports car whipped by with the personalized license plate that read, "Teach Em." I remember crying out to the LORD saying I wanted to teach them, but I did not have the five thousand dollars to purchase necessary equipment. The LORD spoke to my heart, just as clearly as if He were right by my side: *"How serious are you? Will you fast?"* I spoke out loud and said, *"I will do anything."* I think sometimes we just need to wrestle with the LORD and show Him that we mean business!

> (24) And Jacob was left alone; and there wrestled a man with him until the breaking of the day. (25) And when he saw that he prevailed not against him, he touched the hollow of his thigh; and the hollow of Jacob's thigh was out of joint, as he wrestled with him. (26) And he said, Let me go, for the day breaketh. And he said, I will not let thee go, except thou bless me. (27) And he said unto him, What is thy name? And he said, Jacob. (28) And he said, Thy name shall be called no more Jacob, but Israel: for as a prince hast thou power with God and with men, and hast prevailed. (29) And Jacob asked him, and said, Tell me, I pray thee, thy name. And he said, Wherefore is it that thou dost ask after my name? And he blessed him there. *(Genesis 32:24-30)*

Jacob wrestled with God and held on until he received his blessing. The LORD knows the thoughts and intents of our hearts, but the act of seeking Him through fasting brings Him pleasure by displaying that we are willing to seek Him in the manner He has designed. In his book *Fasting Your Way to Health,* J. Harold Smith said, "The Bible teaches fasting." [78] He also said, "Fasting is a discipline that is pleasing to the Father." [79]

I knew nothing of fasting; all I knew was that I had committed to the LORD not to eat anything until I had the five thousand dollars or forty-days, whichever came first. At that time, I weighed one hundred and sixty-five pounds soaking wet; I did not think there would be anything left of me in forty-days, but I was on my way.

I do not necessarily recommend that you go on a cold turkey fast like I did, especially if you have health problems. I knew nothing about the physical ramifications fasting has on the body, nor did I understand how it could affect it. All I knew was the LORD was moving, and I was following.

I stopped in Columbia, South Carolina, to visit my little brother, Mark, on the way home. While I was at his house, I began to call some of my preacher friends to ask them to help me raise the money for the equipment. Once again, I was ushered into the presence of God. He spoke to my heart and said, *"Are you going to trust your preacher friends or Me?"* I put the phone down and prayed. I do not remember the exact details of the next seventeen days, but, to make a long story short, seventeen days later I had five thousand dollars in one hand and a biscuit in the other! Glory to His holy name! For the record, this powerpoint projector was the very first one in the Rock of Ages Ministries. This marvelous display of God's provision marked the beginning of my fasting days.

God has blessed our Prison Prevention ministry with a great team of men and ladies who are currently very actively working in many public schools in America. We have a tremendous curriculum that has been developed and is being widely used in other countries as well. I am not taking credit for any of this work, but I do wonder what may have come of the public school ministry had God not instructed me to fast.

Soon after this seventeen-day fast, the LORD directed me to my first forty-day fast. I was staying in a prophet's chamber in Atoka, Tennessee, while working in a prison revival. I had been pleading with the LORD in prayer for relief concerning my wife's headaches. At that time, Paula, my wife, had been suffering with a daily headache for over fifteen years. This is when some will ask how long we have been married. I agree, I am one of her headaches, but I am not going away, and it appeared as if her physical headaches were not either.

We had exhausted just about every possible medical treatment by this time. While I was in my devotions that morning, I read about Hezekiah asking God for fifteen more years of life after he became deathly ill. The LORD heard and answered, "Turn again, and tell Hezekiah the captain of my people, Thus saith the LORD, the God of David thy father, I have heard thy prayer, I have seen thy tears: behold, I will heal thee: on the third day thou shalt go up unto the house of the LORD" *(2 Kings 20:5)*. I got really excited because it seemed as if the LORD was telling me He was going to heal my wife on the third day. I knew the third day was significant in what God was telling me, but I was unsure of what it implied. When I asked Him what the "third day" meant, He simply spoke to my heart with His reply: *"The first day was the day she was born, the second the day she was born again, and the third day when she comes home to Glory."* This was not the answer I wanted to hear! Almost immediately my mind went to the passage in the Bible where Moses sought the LORD to change His mind. I, too, sought the LORD for forty days trying to get Him to change His mind and heal my darling wife.

> (9) And the LORD said unto Moses, I have seen this people, and, behold, it is a stiffnecked people: (10) Now therefore let me alone, that my wrath may wax hot against them, and that I may consume them: and I will make of thee a great nation. (11) And Moses besought the LORD his God, and said,

LORD, why doth thy wrath wax hot against thy people, which thou hast brought forth out of the land of Egypt with great power, and with a mighty hand? (12) Wherefore should the Egyptians speak, and say, For mischief did he bring them out, to slay them in the mountains, and to consume them from the face of the earth? Turn from thy fierce wrath, and repent of this evil against thy people. (13) Remember Abraham, Isaac, and Israel, thy servants, to whom thou swarest by thine own self, and saidst unto them, I will multiply your seed as the stars of heaven, and all this land that I have spoken of will I give unto your seed, and they shall inherit it for ever. (14) And the LORD repented of the evil which he thought to do unto his people. *(Exodus 32:9-14)*

My wife and I will have been married for thirty years April 16, 2013. We continue to pray and ask God to heal the horrible headaches she suffers, but are content to understand that His grace is sufficient! "And he said unto me, My grace is sufficient for thee: for my strength is made perfect in weakness. Most gladly therefore will I rather glory in my infirmities, that the power of Christ may rest upon me" *(2 Corinthians 12:9)*. We have had the elders of our church come together to pray and anoint her with oil according to James 5:14, 15: "(14) Is any sick among you? let him call for the elders of the church; and let them pray over him, anointing him with oil in the name of the LORD: (15) And the prayer of faith shall save the sick, and the LORD shall raise him up; and if he have committed sins, they shall be forgiven him." Paula and I have exercised all of the spiritual avenues God records in His Word and are content to live with His answer.

I will say this again and again throughout this book; you are in no way, shape, or form going to back God into a corner and force Him to answer your prayer the way you want. Your fast will give Him the liberty to answer it the way He desires, and your obedience will give you the perfect peace to accept His answer!

Fasting became a way of life for me. I began to fast one twenty-four-hour period a week for eight years, give or take a month or two. Many times the LORD would call me to ten-day fasts, three-day fasts, or sometimes I would not stop until I heard from Him.

One time I was fasting for my son as he was about to graduate and go off to college. I did not know how long; I just knew the LORD would tell me when to stop. I was reading in the book of Psalms that morning and came across this verse: "The LORD hath heard my supplication; the LORD will receive my prayer" *(Psalm 6:9)*. Praise the LORD! I knew God had heard my prayer, and to go longer would have been nothing but a hunger strike.

Use your Scripture to call you to fast, to teach you during your fast, and to determine the length of your fast: "Order my steps in thy word: and let not any iniquity have dominion over me" *(Psalm 119:133)*. You will be amazed how the Bible can become alive when you are seeking guidance through His Words.

As previously discussed, fasting can be a very dry and desolate time as well. Please do not seek some "experience" with God because you are fasting. We must always understand that we are to live by faith in this age and not by sight or by some emotional feeling.

The use of your Scripture is vitally important when fasting. It is fascinating to experience the way God will speak to your heart to guide and direct you through your fast with His Word. Seventeen days into my first forty-day fast I asked the LORD if I could drink juice for the remaining twenty-three days. The very next day, I was visiting with a pastor friend; he asked me to look over some Sunday school curriculum he was considering using. As I glanced through the pages, I came across this verse: "Drink no longer water, but use a little wine for thy stomach's sake and thine often infirmities" *(1 Timothy 5:23)*. I remember chuckling, thanking the LORD, and getting some juice. Just for the record, it is not a good idea to put apple juice on an empty stomach! I am sure it is different for each individual, but grape juice seems to be the best answer.

When you make a commitment to the LORD, please do not break your vow. There is a clear example of this given to us when a prophet of God delivered a message to the king. He was then summoned to eat with the king but gave this response:

> (8) And the man of God said unto the king, If thou wilt give me half thine house, I will not go in with thee, neither will I eat bread nor drink water in this place: (9) For so was it charged me by the word of the LORD, saying, Eat no bread, nor drink water, nor turn again by the same way that thou camest. *(I Kings 13:8, 9)*

Another prophet heard of his work and asked him over for supper. The prophet again gave his call of God and said he would not eat. What happened next is a sad commentary but leaves us with the example to obey God, not man: "He said unto him, I am a prophet also as thou art; and an angel spake unto me by the word of the LORD, saying, Bring him back with thee into thine house, that he may eat bread and drink water. But he lied unto him" *(I Kings 13:18)*. He believed the lie, had the meal, and was killed because he allowed the other prophet to talk him into breaking his commitment to the LORD. "When thou vowest a vow unto God, defer not to pay it; for he hath no pleasure in fools: pay that which thou hast vowed" *(Ecclesiastes 5:4).* You do not have to set a specific time, but if God directs into a specific outline for your fast and you agree, you had better keep your end of the deal! Rest assured God will keep His end! You can ask God through Scripture to reveal to you a start and finish time. His Word is alive, and He will show you start and finish times.

Another fast the LORD directed me in was a fast for a close friend of the family who was dying of cancer. My family and I entered into what is called the "Esther Fast." It is a Complete Fast from both food and water for three days. Joshua, Paula, and I made it all three days, and Jessica only went a little over a day. I had talked with our friend on a number of different occasions about his soul. He was a Jewish man and was quite satisfied with his religion. Although he never publicly told us he accepted Christ, shortly after his death, they found a calendar in his room where he had penned in two different places that Jesus Christ is King! It sounds to me like he was saved: "Wherefore I give you to understand, that no man speaking by the Spirit of God calleth Jesus accursed: and that no man can say that Jesus is the LORD, but by the Holy Ghost" *(1 Corinthians 12:3).* Only Heaven will reveal if he made it or not, but our family did our part on his behalf. The question God posed to me in my first fast comes to mind. How serious are you about your lost loved ones?

One of the hardest decisions I have been faced with in my life was to move from the Juvenile Team to the Foreign Department. Brother Rick and Sister Hildebrand are two of my closest friends on the planet. Brother Hildebrand is the director of the juvenile work in America. Together we worked diligently to build the Juvenile Team into what it is today. In my heart I wanted things to be the same; however, the LORD was showing me the world full of teens that needed our help. God used Psalm 2:8 to show me the youth of the world: "Ask of me, and I shall give thee the heathen for thine inheritance, and the uttermost parts of the earth for thy possession." I have penned down this note beside this verse in my Bible: please give me the youth of the world!

The LORD, once again, directed me to fast to be confident it was His will for this direction. I had counseled and preached many times that to prepare for a ministry we should get alone with God and fast as Christ gave us His example. After Christ was baptized and the Holy Ghost descended on Him like a dove, He entered into the wilderness to fast and pray.

(1) And Jesus being full of the Holy Ghost returned from

Jordan, and was led by the Spirit into the wilderness, (2) Being forty days tempted of the devil. And in those days he did eat nothing: and when they were ended, he afterward hungered. *(Luke 4:1, 2)*

I knew I needed to practice what I preached. The Bible says that Christ did not eat anything and was hungry at the conclusion of the fast. This leads me to believe that He did drink water and He did not use the supernatural powers He, God in the flesh, could have used.

Notice that Jesus went into the wilderness "...full of the Holy Ghost..." and at the conclusion of this season of fasting, we see Him returning in the "POWER" of the Holy Spirit: "And Jesus returned in the power of the Spirit into Galilee: and there went out a fame of him through all the region round about" *(Luke 4:14)*. We know, as born-again Christians, the blessed Holy Ghost of God dwells in us. But there is a big difference in being full of the Holy Ghost and having the power of the Holy Ghost! This passage gives us the grounds to believe that it was the forty-day fast that released the Holy Ghost's power to work in His ministry. There is no doubt in my mind that a ministry that includes fasting will trigger the blessed Holy Ghost to work in marvelous ways.

In His weak physical state, Jesus used the Word of God to fight off the devil in each of the three temptations. Our Bible is the most important possession and weapon we have: "No weapon that is formed against thee shall prosper; and every tongue that shall rise against thee in judgment thou shalt condemn. This is the heritage of the servants of the LORD, and their righteousness is of me, saith the LORD" *(Isaiah 54:17)*.

It was my desire to know for sure that I was in God's perfect will, and I knew this fast would confirm it and empower it. I was forty-seven years old at the time and still in good heath. Reminded of the advice Dr. Gearis gave to do it while I was young and in good health, I entered into a forty-day Water-Only Fast to seek God's direct approval on the international work.

It was the thirty-third day the LORD gave me 2 Timothy 4:5 to confirm His call: "But watch thou in all things, endure afflictions, do the work of an evangelist, make full proof of thy ministry." My prayers were answered in full; I knew what He had led me to do. I have a place marked in my Bible that I can go back to when the devil starts hurling fiery darts at me, trying to get me to quit or to stumble and fall, a place where the LORD gave me peace about what He would have me to do.

On the twenty-seventh day of this fast, our family dropped into a church in the neighboring town for the mid-week service. The preacher preached out of a passage in Ecclesiastes: "Behold that which I have seen: it is good and comely for one to eat and to drink, and to enjoy the good of all his labour that he taketh under the sun all the days of his life, which God giveth him: for it is his portion" *(Ecclesiastes 5:18)*. My daughter, Jessica, and my wife, Paula, both looked at me and said that they thought God was telling me to eat. I smiled and reminded them of my verse the LORD used to call for the fast: "Is not this the fast that I have chosen? to loose the bands of wickedness, to undo the heavy burdens, and to let the oppressed go free, and that ye break every yoke" *(Isaiah 58:6)*? However, I did pen in my Bible that I believed the LORD had given me clear direction to end my fasting for extended periods as well as the day-a-week fast once I had completed this fast! I am sure He is satisfied with my desire to seek His strength in my weakness! I thank Him and praise Him! I will fast when the LORD directs me, but as far as weekly and for extended periods, I feel as if He has said it is enough!

A forty-day Water-Only Fast is very difficult. The last five days proved to be more difficult than I ever imagined. I knew God would sustain me; but physically, emotionally, and even spiritually, I was drained. I was not drinking enough water, and I began to dehydrate. I did not realize this until the paramedics explained to me how the body reacts during the dehydration period. Each time I would try to drink water, my body would reject it, and I would vomit.

I was thirty-eight and one-half days into the fast, and by now I kept a glass of water nearby at all times. I would drink some water and then head to the bathroom every couple of hours. It was late in the evening, and I was considering going to bed. My wife took my water back to our room, but I remained on the couch and fell asleep. I awoke suddenly needing water, but it was not there. When I jumped up to go to the refrigerator for some cold water, I passed out. I was reminded by my daughter, after I came to in her arms, that I told the LORD I would only go as long as I physically could. For the last day and a half, I drank some juice and broth. A lesson learned by experience is any sudden movement can cause dizziness and loss of consciousness during a fast.

As you can see, fasting has been a part of our lives for many years. It is my desire to proclaim to all who will listen that fasting is a wonderful way to walk with God and to tap into His power. I do not completely understand why He wants us to go through the fasting process, but who am I to wonder?

It is a good idea to keep a detailed journal during your fasting. I was not very good at this for most of my fasting, but, regardless of my failure, it is a good idea. In his book, Dr. J. Harold Smith gives a chart that recorded his weight and a brief description of his daily activities during one of his fasts.[80] You can also find a detailed diary of a twenty-one day fast in chapter 22 of Arthur Wallis' book *God's Chosen Fast.*[81] I did keep a journal on the forty-day fast for the international work. I missed a few days in the beginning, and the last eight days are not recorded. Reading back through your experience is a tremendous help. I have included my journal at the end of the book if you would like to see what I experienced. I wish that I had finished it, but what I did record has helped me when I have reviewed it. The last two days are easy to remember. I spent the thirty-eighth day very sick. It was late that night when I passed out and began drinking some juice. The thirty-ninth day was a day of rest and preparation for the upcoming revival the next day. The fortieth day I drove from my home in Murfreesboro, Tennessee, to Bowden, Georgia, to begin a prison revival in a juvenile facility in Atlanta, Georgia.

During my trip to Bowden, I broke my fast with a banana and some vegetables. The next few days I ate cooked vegetables to ease my system back into eating. As a result of my fast, I have total peace knowing the LORD wants me to continue my work on the international field. In the book *How to Fast Successfully,* Derek Prince made the statement that he believed that fasting helped settle his course of life and ministry. [82]

There are over ten million inmates around the world who need to hear the Good News that Jesus saves! There are also many public school students whom we will introduce to Christ through our labors. By His grace and through His power, we hope and pray to accomplish great things for the cause of Christ as we labor together with Him!

Brother Chris Hooker joined the Rock of Ages Ministry in December, 1992, and he served as the Florida state director. On the morning of February 8, 2002, Brother Chris left his home to conduct a prison revival in a Florida prison. Two miles from his home a nineteen-year-old young man in a pickup truck ran a stop sign and broadsided Brother Chris's van. The collision forced Brother Chris into a log truck that was in the left turn lane on the opposite side of the four-lane road. The driver of the pickup truck was left uninjured, but his passenger was not so fortunate. He did not survive the accident. Brother Chris was the only one in his vehicle. He was not expected to live, but the LORD was not yet finished with him. Just before his accident he had asked the LORD to allow him to do greater things in the next ten years of his ministry than he had done in the beginning, but now his dreams seemed to be shattered.

Shortly after Brother Chris's accident, the LORD impressed me to begin a Partial Fast from drinking coffee as a reminder to pray for him. I told the LORD I would not drink another cup of coffee until Brother Chris could walk. The injuries have left him paralyzed from the neck down with just a little movement in one of his arms. I can honestly say, next to my family, I have never prayed for another man and his family more than I have prayed for Brother Chris. Even the smell or the thought of coffee reminds me to take him before the throne of God.

After his accident, he served as the secretary/treasurer of our ministry for many years and now is a representative raising financial and prayer support for the work. The LORD has allowed him to begin a ministry called Treasure Investors.

My children know why I am not drinking coffee any longer. On occasion I would make a comment like, "Boy, that coffee smells good." Jessica, my daughter, would say to me, "You better pray, Daddy." Like Queen Esther, you can rest assured when trouble comes by my little girl's way she will know how to reach God.

My children have lived in a home where fasting was practiced. I included them in my fasts by sharing with them what God was doing. Many times they would ask me what God did that day and were excited when I would share the blessing. I have been pleased to see my children enter into fasts of their own when personal needs arose in their lives.

I preached a message on fasting in the Gospel Light Baptist Church in Heber Springs, Arkansas, and made mention of the Partial Fast I was doing for Brother Chris. A few days later I saw the youth pastor from the Gospel Light Baptist Church at another meeting. He told me a young lady in the youth department decided to fast from soft drinks until the youth pastor's wife became pregnant. They had been asking God for a baby for three years but had still not been successful. I was thrilled to hear that someone was going to put to practice what she had learned.

I was on my way to another revival and stopped off at a small church that allowed me to use their camper in the parking lot for a few days. I remember praying and thanking God that this teenager was willing to put to action a Biblical principle she had learned on behalf of her youth pastor. In my prayer time, the LORD impressed me to enter into her fast with her. I, too, began to fast from cokes: "Again I say unto you, That if two of you shall agree on earth as touching any thing that they shall ask, it shall be done for them of my Father which is in heaven" *(Matthew 18:19)*. The LORD so impressed me that He would answer this prayer that He moved me to send them a letter to inform them of my prayer meeting. God told me that they would be with child in one month's time. With some hesitation, I wrote the letter and sent it.

Three weeks later, I was in a prison revival meeting at our annual Florida Blitz when my phone rang. On the other end of the phone was the youth pastor and my friend Claud Slate. He started telling me about how God had been blessing the youth group and other small talk, and then he said, "Oh yeah, Abby is pregnant." Claud and Abby Slate are proud parents of little Addison Faith Slate. God has also added two more little girls, Ava and Aubrey, and a son, Claud Hassel III, to their family. Glory to God in the highest! At least two other babies are in this world because of this teenager's testimony in the power of fasting. These are referred to as Partial Fasts.

There was a great revival going on in the teen department at Franklin Road Christian School in Murfreesboro, Tennessee. Brother Kurt Copeland is the youth pastor and in charge of scheduling chapel speakers. I am privileged to be a part of the preachers who influence these students. Because of the hunger for God and His power displayed by the students, I was impressed to preach to them in chapel on fasting. A little over a year later, one of the teen girls who was in the service saw me and shared this testimony. She said that she had a close friend who had lost two or more children to miscarriages. She told her friend that she would not eat any candy as a Partial Fast until she had a healthy baby. Not long after, this lady conceived and gave birth to a healthy baby, and God gets the glory! This girl was so excited to share with me how God had answered her season of fasting.

One family in a church in Ohio was not able to have children. After hearing the message on fasting, they sought God through fasting and prayer and now have a healthy baby boy today, and God gets the glory!

After preaching on fasting in the First Baptist Church of Germantown, Ohio, Lisa Litteral sought the LORD to find out whether she should have more children or not; God gave her the answer. She gave the number of children they would have to the LORD!

Brother Jamie Doss, who is with our Juvenile Team, has not drunk a soft drink for years now; he has a burden for the healing of my dear wife's headaches and considers his fast a way of praying for God's grace with Paula's health! Jamie is a true Christian friend!

"Fasting is a form of worship and communication with the LORD separate from prayer…. It gives the LORD a sense of urgency in your request and shows Him your total confidence in the teachings of His precious Word, the KING JAMES BIBLE."

My last forty-day fast started on Thursday, April 16, 2009. I finished my last meal at approximately 7:30 p.m. I weighed in at 181 pounds.

The first full day Paula and Jess left to go to Ohio, leaving me by myself. After our morning meeting for prayer with the men, I came home and helped Paula and Jess load the truck. They were off at 7:00 a.m. I then went to my office and worked there for three or four hours. Already very weak, I spent the rest of the day resting and reading. I had a desire to at least read the entire New Testament through a few times during my fast. My desire was to draw close to my Saviour and to receive a special touch from Him. I wrote in my journal that I need to have better spiritual understanding of the Scriptures and am seeking Him for this. I also have a desire to seek His face in the efforts in the Philippines. I am not sure of all that will be required of me, but I am willing to do whatever I can. I am also asking our Saviour for the financial relief that we will need to make these extra trips. I know it is going to be a burden on our family, and I only want Paula to have peace. I am excited about this fast, but I also know that it will be very difficult. I thank my Saviour for teaching me this awesome way of fellowshipping with Him!

Day 2, April 18 - Weighed in at 175 pounds. Today I was up at 6:00 and prayed for a while. I then went to the church for the prayer breakfast. I continued my day working at the church (Franklin Road Baptist Church, Murfreesboro, TN) in preparation for the grand opening of our new building. I was there until around 8:30 that evening. It was a difficult day, but the LORD gave me grace each step of the way. What a joy it is to work on the house of God! We are praying that the LORD will fill our buildings up with three thousand or more. I know He can do it. After I arrived home, I read a few chapters in Matthew, and my Paula called. It is always good to hear her voice. I then slipped off to sleep.

Day 3, April 19, 2009 - Up and ready for church by 7:30. Out in my office and checking e-mails. By writing this note I see that I am not really spending enough time directly with Jesus. The computer can take my time from me although I use it for Him. I did not write my devotions for the last two days, and I need to send these people a thought. Please LORD let me use these forty days to walk directly beside You so You can instruct me! If there is any sin in my life that you need to deal with, please let me know! I love You, LORD Jesus, and I only want to serve you to the fullest! Please also take care of this high blood pressure issue for me. Watch over my Jessica, Joshua, and Sarah. Use my children for Your honor and glory! Please, LORD, help my wife's health, also. She really hurts and needs a touch of Your grace. They will be driving home from Ohio today, and I need you to watch over them as they travel. I am sure you will bring them home to me safely! I love you, LORD!

Day 10, April 26, 2009 - I am very weak and do not feel good. We are in revival at the United States Disciplinary Barracks in Ft. Leavenworth, Kansas. During our break, I listened to Dr. Gibbs preach a message on our weakness and His strength. With tears running down my face, I told the LORD that I was too weak to do this and I must rely on His strength! Please LORD allow me Your power to finish this fast! I love you, LORD, and only want to see the world reached for Your dear Son!

Day 11, April 27 - I flew from Kansas City to Nashville then drove to Culpepper, Virginia. I chewed on ice most of the way. My stomach felt a little better, but I am still unable to just drink a bottle of water without feeling badly. Met a man at a gas station who is an Independent Baptist. I believe he will become one of my prayer warriors. Made it safely! What a day! I listened to some preaching on the radio. I need the LORD so badly to help me draw so close to Him that I can feel His breath! I love the LORD!

Day 12, April 28, 2009 - It has now been twelve days of water-only fasting. This morning while I was reading a book on the physical benefits of fasting by Paul Bragg, I came across a verse: "Therefore go thou, and read in the roll, which thou hast written from my mouth, the words of the LORD in the ears of the people in the LORD's house upon the fasting day: and also thou shalt read them in the ears of all Judah that come out of their cities" *(Jeremiah 36:6)*. There is a great value in reading His Word all the time, but I now see the importance of reading it during this fast. Thursday I will be driving for close to fifteen hours. I have made plans to listen to the New Testament on tape.

I have found it very difficult keeping hydrated. My mouth seems to always be dry. It is hard to drink water because I seem to have a lump in my throat. I do not ever remember having this problem before. My blood pressure was 147/95 today. My heart seems to be beating out of my chest. I have been at the altar a time or two today seeking God's power, provisions, and his direction in the Philippine ministry. I feel as if I have not had a great closeness to God during this fast so far. I told the LORD today that I was not expecting a great vision or movement, I just wanted Him to be pleased with my fast. Every time I question Him concerning my blood pressure He reminds me of one of the verses He used early in the fast: "Is not this the fast that I have chosen? to loose the bands of wickedness, to undo the heavy burdens, and to let the oppressed go free, and that ye break every yoke" *(Isaiah 58:6)*? My prayer tonight is that He would allow me the strength to endure this fast for His glory and my good.

Day 13, April 29, 2009 - I woke up today without having such a dry mouth. The LORD has heard and answered this prayer. We are about to finish the last service of our coordinators' meeting. I feel a little weak; but, for the most part, I feel pretty good. I praise the LORD for the strength He has given me through these first thirteen days.

Day 14, April 30, 2009 - Drove all day and listened to the four Gospels on cassette. It is important to make the Word of God a part of your fast. I wish I could say I have engulfed myself in it, but it seems very difficult for me to read. I still am having a hard time with my swallowing, and this is causing a lot of discomfort. I know that this is all part of the special time I have chosen to seek God. Last night the LORD answered my request; six were saved in the last service. It was a wonderful night. I arrived safely around 8:30 p.m. in Tallahassee. Praise the LORD for His safety!

Day 15, May 1, 2009 - Brother Paul Carver asked me to do the Prison Presentation powerpoint lesson in the first part of the services at Leon Regional Juvenile Detention Center (RJDC). I must say that the LORD always empowers me when He has me to stand and preach His Word. It was amazing to me how the Spirit of God moved in the service. For three hours I was able to warn the kids of the dangers this world has to offer, while presenting Christ as the answer to all their problems! At the conclusion of the service, somewhere around ten hands went in the air professing that they trusted the LORD! In my weakness, He is strong. I was exhausted and rested for about an hour before we had to go back in for the evening service.

Day 16, May 2, 2009 - I am still very weak and tired. We counseled with the students at the RJDC for almost three hours and then went back to the room. I once again found myself resting. Many times throughout the day I am talking to the LORD. I know He is there. Brother Paul asked me to preach the evening service, and once again God moved. I changed my message in the first five minutes, and, my, how He worked! Three were saved in the services. Praise His name!

Day 17, May 3, 2009 - We concluded our revival at Leon RJDC. Nikki, a thirteen-year-old girl, told me that God was calling her into the ministry; what a joy! The team made its way over to Gospel Light Baptist Church where Brother Clark asked me to give an update. It amazes me how the LORD empowers me and fills my mouth with the words to speak to His people. I then drove to Lake Butler where I met with Pastor Tim Ellison concerning Prison Prevention in his area. Praise the LORD, he is willing. Brother Jowers, Pastor of Grace Baptist Church in Baldwin, Florida, bought me a room for the night. I spent the evening reading on fasting by Bragg and then talking to my family on the phone. It seems very difficult to spend a long period of prayer on my face. Still not really sure why this is, but I asked the LORD last night to show me His glory! I so desire to know that He is pleased with the time of fasting I have set aside for Him. I thank Him for allowing me this opportunity!

Day 18, May 4, 2009 - I spent the morning with Brother Jowers. He has a son who is out in the world. We had a good talk, and he gave me some awesome advice as I described my difficulty in prayer. He told me that sometimes God does not want us to say anything but just listen. I think I have been so busy and consumed with begging Him for His power and direction that He just wants me to hush. I drove for six hours to Panama City without listening to anything. I had a few phone calls, but for the most part I just drove. I still want His power and approval on my ministry! I arrived at Heritage Boys' Home and will preach devotions for the evening! I just plan on bragging on the LORD!

Day 19, May 5, 2009 - It is still not getting any easier as my fast progresses. I preached the morning and evening devotion to the boys with a true hand of God on each message. Tonight I preached the U.S. Air Force message and had about ten boys stand to take the oath. I know the devil will work harder and harder on them than even before. I am not as sleepy tired as in the past, but my physical stamina is slowly diminishing. I walked around the pond this morning and just tried to be still. The LORD is working on me, but there is no overwhelming sense of His presence other than pure faith that He is with me. I am drawing totally from His strength as I progress from day to day.

Day 20, May 6, 2009 - Wednesday morning is the last day I will be preaching both morning and evening for the boys. Tomorrow starts our Rock of Ages revival at the Bay Regional Detention Center. Brother Carver will be holding the meetings and calling the preachers. I walked around the pond again this morning just seeking the LORD for His grace. I have not been sleeping very long, but I seem to be getting enough rest to carry me through the day. I went down to the pond a couple of hours before the evening service to just meditate on the message a little. I began to untangle a knot that was in the two cane fishing poles on the dock. As I untangled the knotted-up mess, the LORD showed me some real truths about how slow the process can sometimes be of getting right with the LORD. As we allow Him to loosen knot by knot, before long we will have a tangle-free life: just a little nugget by the pond from the LORD! After the evening service, I was physically exhausted. It was a true blessing to be able to see Brother Chris Heyder again. He is home and right with the LORD.

Day 21, May 7, 2009 - Up early and down by the pond again. I am still very weak and just relying totally on Him for strength. Went to RJDC with the team, and Brother Paul allowed me to preach to the girls. I will say this, it seems as if I have great power in the pulpit as I am preaching. In-between services I went to the room and took a forty-five minute nap. The rest was good. After the evening service, Brother Chris and I went out; I bought him supper. It is good to see him home.

Day 22, May 8, 2009 - I drove from Panama City to New Orleans to pick up Paula. It was good to see my bride. I listened to the book of John on tape, and the LORD really showed me a truth when He was asking Peter if he loved Him. The first time He told him to feed my lambs – little children; the second time, feed my sheep – middle-aged; the third time, He was talking about what manner of death He would die – senior saints. Paula and I had supper with Pastor Silvertooth and his family. We had a good time. I explained my fast to him, and I know he will be praying!

Day 23, May 9, 2009 - Today I feel very weak and not very good in my stomach and head. I went on visitation because that is what the LORD would have me do. He allowed me to win a teenager to Christ. Paula is giving her testimony tonight. Very, very weak and wishing I could eat. By His strength, I will finish this fast. I am losing a lot of weight and really beginning to look sickly.

Day 24, Sunday, May 10, 2009 - It is not getting any easier to continue this fast. The LORD continues to remind me that this is the chosen fast He has for me. I know that He is in total control as I rely on Him for my strength. He has given me favor in the pulpit every time I preach. I hope and pray that this power will continue long after my fast is completed. I preached to the teens in Sunday school on a reason to live. There are a few boys who are messing around with sin, and I am very concerned for them. Oh, how I wish they could just learn to trust the LORD! We had lunch at Brother Rusty's. Paula had a good time with the ladies. I really missed out on a great meal there for the glory of GOD! I preached the message the LORD has given me on

His power by our burden. It seems like the LORD used the message, and I hope He did. We will need His power to continue on with our trips. I had a hard time sleeping. My mouth is so very dry; it is almost impossible to receive any relief from it.

Day 25, Monday, May 11, 2009 - Up around 6:30 to walk and read some of John Maxwell's book *Failing Forward*. It is a very good book. I took Brother Charles Harding to breakfast and had a great talk with him. This man is very intelligent concerning America. I trust the LORD will use him as He tries to get America to wake up to prayer. Paula and I will spend some time together today. We picked up Jessica's bed. I am so glad the LORD has allowed me to get her a very nice bed. Brother Mike Powell then took us out to eat lunch at the Bass Pro Shop. I had a great talk with him. He really loves the LORD and wants to be used. Paula then went back to Dana's to get her hair permed. I was very weak and tired. After talking with Brother Felix for a while, I went and took a short nap. We then went over to Clyde and Luraleen's so Paula could have supper. I sure do love those folks. Back to the room to pack and prepare for tomorrow's trip.

Day 26, Tuesday, May 12, 2009 - By now my throat is completely hoarse. It seems as if I am getting the drainage from the back of my throat causing me to lose my voice. I did not talk much while driving, and Paula slept a lot. My mouth is so very dry no matter how much I drink or do not drink. We arrived home at 4:30 or so. Ted picked me up, and we went to see Brother Joey at the hospital. He surely did not look very good. We had prayer and came home.

Day 27, Wednesday, May 13, 2009 - I went to church at Rutherford County Baptist Church, Pastor Chisgar. My voice is still very bad. The LORD gave me a very clear mind as I gave the testimony of how He has and is using us in the ministry. I praise His name. It was very funny tonight at church. The preacher preached out of Ecclesiastes chapter 3 where the Bible says, "It is good for a man to eat and drink!" Sis and Paula both looked at me and said that they think God is telling me to eat. I smiled and told them my verse! "Is this not the fast I have chosen for you?" I did pen in my Bible that I believe the LORD has given me clear direction to end my fasting for extended periods as well as the day-a-week fast! I am sure He is satisfied with my desire to seek His strength in my weakness! I thank Him and praise Him!

Day 28, Thursday, May 14, 2009 - This morning I preached at the Franklin Road Christian School to the entire student body that was present. I had the lower classmen from 8:15 until 9:15 and then the teens from 10:10 to 11:05 or so. I preached on righteousness! It was a great message the LORD gave me. I just hope they took it to heart. After chapel, Paula and I went to the VA hospital clinic to have me checked out. I still have fluid on the ear causing the drainage, and they wanted me on an antibiotic. I told the lady, who is a member of our church, that I was fasting and did not want to take anything right now. She said it is going to be a rough twelve days but I would survive. If she only knew how rough the first twenty-eight have been! The LORD is so good to me; I do not deserve to even be in His presence! I am still kind of in a spiritual lull if you will! I know He is helping me endure this very hard time. We picked up a Little Caesar's pizza to bring home for the girls. I sure did enjoy smelling it. I then went outside and trimmed up a bunch of the bushes. I do not know how I am able to even move as weak as I am! It is Him!

Day 29, Friday, May 15, 2009 - I ordered eight pizzas for the eighth grade class for passing out the most tracts. It was a joy to see them eat all that pizza and chips and drink all the pop. I gave them a short devotion out of Proverbs 8:19-21. It was a good time. I then came home, changed my clothes, and went back to the bus garage to change my transmission fluid. After I finished with the truck, I then went to get my mower to fix it. All it needed was a spark plug; praise the LORD! I was very tired and weak! I threw up some junk at the bus barn bathroom then went home and rested. I watched a video about the Elliot family, missionaries. What an inspiration to see how the LORD used them! Still seeking the LORD to show me His glory. It just may be I need to find the wilderness! I made Paula some supper with the sausage I got from LA and then made a stew in the crockpot. It sure does smell good!

Day 30, Saturday, May 16, 2009 - I did not get much sleep last night. I was up early (6:15) and drove half way to meet Brother David Taft to deliver 375 Ultimate Truth New Testaments for a public school. We had a good talk; I then drove home and picked up all the sticks in the yard. I also set up the full-size bed in the spare room. I made Paula supper. Ted came over, and we chipped up all the sticks from the yard. While driving, I listened to the books of Acts and part of Romans on the tape player. I am still kind of confused on the lack of my spirit interacting with the LORD during this fast. It seems as if I am just physically existing and not really spending time in prayer. It is so difficult to concentrate, to read, or study because of the hunger and weakness. It could be He just wants me to endure and continue trusting in His strength during my weakness! All I know is that if I am going to make it, I must rely completely on His strength. As I write this note, it is 9:39 p.m., and my throat is dry, and I am very hungry. I am not really sleepy, just tired. LORD, I NEED YOU BADLY RIGHT NOW!

Day 31, May 17, 2009 - I had a very difficult night sleeping again. It seems like I have no rest. I woke up many times and just talked to the LORD. Paula and I are very concerned about our finances, which is part of the reason for the fast. If I am going to be able to accomplish this awesome task that the LORD has called me to, I must get my finances in order: Joshua's wedding, the September trip. I NEED HIS HELP! I am asking the LORD to allow Scott to buy my share of the farm. This would be a great help to us! I preached to the bus teens today on truth. There was not a whole lot of response, but it surely was evident that they were listening. I took about a two-hour nap, which I am not sure if it helped or hurt. The evening service was good. I had a lot of people come up and ask if I was all right. I sure do need Him more than ever.

Day 32, May 18, 2009 - I did not even pick up my Bible today other than to read a Proverb to write a devotion. It is so weird! I so badly want to be directly in His presence, but the cares of every day work are really getting to me. I mowed today, and I had to do it in shifts. I am so very weak, and my throat is so dry. I still have so much mucus draining down the back of my throat; it is so very uncomfortable. I sent my devotion out late this evening. Brother Mark Brown sent this note back to me: "Brother Mike, I read this verse and thought of you tonight. I love this: "Then said he unto me, Fear not, Daniel: for from the first day that thou didst set thine heart to understand, and to chasten thyself before thy God, thy words were heard, and I am come for thy words" (Daniel 10:12). God has been listening, my Brother; your words have been heard. Your Brother, Mark." I wept as I read this note and just cried unto the LORD to show me His glory. I so desperately need to go to the wilderness! I need to just go tomorrow and spend some time in the woods. With His help, I will do this!

As I mentioned earlier in the book, this was my last recording in the journal. The next day, day 33, I received my answer from the LORD. It was confirmed in Scripture that I was to move to the international department of the ministry. I was very weak and tired the last week of this fast. I helped Paula with a garage sale but was not able to work for long periods of time. Halfway through the thirty-eighth day, I moved too quickly and passed out. Paula was very concerned and called 911. I told the paramedics that I had been fasting for a long period of time. They told me that I had just moved too quickly. Jessica, my daughter, reminded me that I had told the LORD that I would go until I felt I was in physical danger. After thirty-eight and one-half days of only drinking water, I took in some juice off of oatmeal and some broth from a soup. The thirty-ninth day, I prepared to go to a prison revival in the Atlanta area. On the last day of my fast, I would drive to Bowden, Georgia, to meet with Dr. Ricky Dunsford. The next day, we would begin our three-day revival at the juvenile detention center.

"I feel as if I had just dipped my toe into the pool of power that is fasting, but I'm ready to jump in when the LORD leads."

STEPHANIE TAYLOR

Conclusion

The devil will tell you over and over that whatever you attempt for God will fail. William Carey made this famous statement in 1792, "Expect great things from God; attempt great things for God." God has given us an avenue to tap into His great power so we can accomplish great things for Him: "Ah LORD GOD! behold, thou hast made the heaven and the earth by thy great power and stretched out arm, and there is nothing too hard for thee:" *(Jeremiah 32:17)*. We cannot go down to the discount store to pick up His power; we must do it His way. Discounted faith produces discounted fighting with discounted power! It will take sacrifice, humility, endurance, trust, and faith; but when we seek God His way, we cannot only attempt great things for God, but we can accomplish great things for Him, too!

When you study these great heroes of the faith, you will find out that they spent many days fasting, desiring the power of God on their lives, along with seeking direct answers concerning direction. C.T. Studd fasted for eight days and heard from God that Priscilla Stewart would be his wife. In his letter to her on July 25, 1887, he made this statement, "But here I do say that after eight days spent alone in prayer and fasting, I do believe the LORD has shown me that your determination is wrong and will not stand, and that you yourself will see this presently, if the LORD has not shown you already." [83] She did become his wife! These men had the same Bible we do, the same God we do, the same hardships we do, yet they overcame. They did not have the monopoly on His power; they were men like we are! God wants to use us the same way He used them and will if we seek Him as they did!

"Bring ye all the tithes into the storehouse, that there may be meat in mine house, and prove me now herewith, saith the LORD of hosts, if I will not open you the windows of heaven, and pour you out a blessing, that there shall not be room enough to receive it" *(Malachi 3:10)*. I know this verse is referring to tithing, but the same principle can be applied to all of God's instructions in the Bible: "And ye shall seek me, and find me, when ye shall search for me with all your heart" *(Jeremiah 29:13)*.

Do not allow past failures to prevent you from pressing forward. If you desire His power, protection, provision, and His approval, you must add fasting to your prayer life.

"How serious are you?" seems to be the question at hand. Do you want to see your ministry spring forward to new heights? Do you really want to see your lost loved ones saved? If you mean business, then seek His leading in this area of fasting.

I was told of an old preacher who said, "It was not sex that got Adam and Eve in trouble in the garden; it was food that got them!" Food has become the god of this world: "Whose end is destruction, whose God is their belly, and whose glory is in their shame, who mind earthly things" *(Philippians 3:19).*

As we see the last days approaching, the Gospel message is hated more and more. We will need all the power of God we can get to accomplish His work. We must be prepared for "this kind," whatever it is, through prayer and fasting.

As this study has proved, fasting is an integral part of a truly productive relationship with the LORD. Mary gave some great advice when Jesus was about to perform His first earthly miracle: "His mother saith unto the servants, Whatsoever he saith unto you, do it" *(John 2:5).* God gave us His Word to teach us how to be born again, and we believed it. If we take every teaching in His Word to heart like we do eternal life, we will enjoy a victorious and productive Christian life.

End Notes

[1] *Repentance God Save America Conference* – pg. 281 – Gomez Publications – A ministry of Northwest Bible Baptist Church; 9N889 Nesler Road; Elgin, IL 60123

[2] *The Tribune Democrat* – The Shanksville Story – Wednesday, September 11, 2002, pg. 56 – Symbol of Faith, by Tom Lavis

[3] http://www.doesgodexist.org/MarApr98/NoBiblesInJonestown.html

[4] http://www.historycommons.org/timeline.jsp?day_of_9/11=complete_911_timeline_shanksville__pennsylvania&timeline=complete_911_timeline – After 10:06 a.m. September 11, 2001: Paper Debris Survives Flight 93 Crash

[5] http://americanvision.org/3024/flight-93-the-crater-and-the-open-book/

[6] *Heartbeats of the Holy* – pg. 5 – by Keith E. Knauss – Printed by Faith Baptist Publications – Ft. Pierce, FL – http://www.fbcpublications.com

[7] *Heartbeats of the Holy* – pg. 8 – by Keith E. Knauss – Printed by Faith Baptist Publications – Ft. Pierce, FL – http://www.fbcpublications.com

[8] *Shaping History Through Prayer and Fasting* – pg. 139 – by Derek Prince – Derek Prince Ministries; P.O. Box 19501; Charlotte, NC 28219-9501 – ISBN 978-0-88368-773-4

[9] *Shaping History Through Prayer and Fasting* – pg. 32 – by Derek Prince – Derek Prince Ministries; P.O. Box 19501; Charlotte, NC 28219-9501 – ISBN 978-0-88368-773-4

[10] *The Complete Works of Oswald Chambers* – pg. 476 – Discovery House Publishers – ISBN 1-57293-039-X

[11] *Heartbeats of the Holy* – pg. 46 – by Keith E. Knauss – Printed by Faith Baptist Publications – Ft. Pierce, FL – http://www.fbcpublications.com

[12] *Shaping History Through Prayer and Fasting* – pg. 30 – by Derek Prince – Derek Prince Ministries; P.O. Box 19501; Charlotte, NC 28219-9501 – ISBN 978-0-88368-773-4

[13] *The Complete Works of Oswald Chambers* – pg. 2 – Discovery House Publishers – ISBN 1-57293-039-X

[14] *American Dictionary of the English Language* – Noah Webster 1828 – Published by the Foundation for American Christian Education

[15] *Heartbeats of the Holy* – pg. 9 – by Keith E. Knauss – Printed by Faith Baptist Publications – Ft. Pierce, FL – http://www.fbcpublications.com

[16] *Shaping History Through Prayer and Fasting* – pg. 23 – by Derek Prince – Derek Prince Ministries; P.O. Box 19501; Charlotte, NC 28219-9501 – ISBN 978-0-88368-773-4

[17] *http://www.bls.gov/news.release/atus.nr0.htm* - paragraph 13 - World Wide Web

[18] *Heartbeats of the Holy* – pg. 72 – by Keith E. Knauss – Printed by Faith Baptist Publications – Ft. Pierce, FL – http://www.fbcpublications. com

[19] *Heartbeats of the Holy* – pg. 73 – by Keith E. Knauss – Printed by Faith Baptist Publications – Ft. Pierce, FL – http://www.fbcpublications. com

[20] *Treasury of David* – by Charles Spurgeon – Psalm 38:1, 2

[21] *Heartbeats of the Holy* – pg. 90 – by Keith E. Knauss – Printed by Faith Baptist Publications – Ft. Pierce, FL – http://www.fbcpublications. com

[22] *The Man In The Middle* – pg. 34 – by Timothy S. Goeglein – B&H Publishing Group; Nashville, TN – ISBN 978-4336-7288-0

[23] *The Man In The Middle* – pg. 227 – by Timothy S. Goeglein – B&H Publishing Group; Nashville, TN – ISBN 978-4336-7288-0

[24] *The Faith of George W. Bush* – pg. 173 – by Stephen Mansfield –

Charisma House A Strang Company; 600 Rinehart Road; Lake Mary, Florida 32746 – www.charismahouse.com – ISBN 1-59185-242-0

[25] *The Spirit World* – by Richard W. De Haan – http://www.amazon. com/s/ref=nb_sb_noss?url=search-alias%3Dstripbooks&field-keywo rds=the+spirit+world+Richard+W.+De+Haan&x=17&y=21

[26] *Numbers in the Bible* – pg. 77 – by Robert D. Johnston – Kregel Publications, as division of Kregel, Inc.; P.O. box 2607; Grand Rapids, MI 49501 – ISBN 0-8254-2965-x

[27] *Fast Your Way To Health* – pg. 19 – by J. Harold Smith – Radio Bible Hour; P.O. Box 99; Newport, TN 37821– ISBN 0-8407-5776-3

[28] *Fast Your Way To Health* – pg. 104 – by J. Harold Smith – Radio Bible Hour; P.O. Box 99; Newport, TN 37821 – ISBN 0-8407-5776-3

[29] http://showcase.netins.net/web/creative/lincoln/speeches/fast.htm

[30] http://www.usatoday.com/news/religion/2010-04-15-prayer-day_N. htm

[31] http://www.whitehouse.gov/the-press-office/presidential-proclamation-national-day-prayer

[32] http://www.jewishvirtuallibrary.org/jsource/Judaism/esther.html

[33] http://www.ctlibrary.com/ch/1990/issue25/2510.html

[34] *Repentance* – pg. 307 – Gomez Publications – A ministry of Northwest Bible Baptist Church; 9N889   Nesler Road; Elgin, IL 60123

[35] *Repentance* – pg. 318 – Gomez Publications – A ministry of Northwest Bible Baptist Church; 9N889 Nesler Road; Elgin, IL 60123

[36] *Power through Prayer and Fasting* – pg 132 – by Ronnie W. Floyd – Broadman and Holman Publishers – ISBN0-8054-0164-4

[37] *Fast Your Way To Health* – pg. 104 – by J. Harold Smith – Radio Bible Hour; P.O. Box 99; Newport, TN 37821 – ISBN 0-8407-5776-3

[38] *How to fast Successfully* – pg. 37 – by Derek Prince – Derek Prince Ministries—International; P.O. Box 19501; Charlotte, NC 28219 –

ISBN-13: 978-0-88368-345-3

[39] *Numbers in the Bible* – pg. 55 – by Robert D. Johnston – Kregel Publications, as division of Kregel, Inc.; P.O. box 2607; Grand Rapids, MI 49501 – ISBN 0-8254-2965-x

[40] *Experiencing The Depths Of Jesus Christ* – Back cover – by Jeanne Guyon – Seed Sowers Publishing; P.O. Box 3317; Jacksonville, FL 32206 – ISBN-0-940232-00-6

[41] *Experiencing The Depths Of Jesus Christ* – pg. 28 – by Jeanne Guyon – Seed Sowers Publishing; P.O. Box 3317; Jacksonville, FL 32206 – ISBN-0-940232-00-6

[42] *The Miracle of Fasting* – inside cover page – by Paul C. Bragg N.D, Ph.D. and Patricia Bragg N.D, Ph.D. – Published in the United States HEALTH SCIENCE; Box 7; Santa Barbara, California 93102 – www. bragg.com - ISBN-13: 978-0-87790-039-9

[43] http://en.wikipedia.org/wiki/Obesity paragraph 4

[44] http://en.wikipedia.org/wiki/Fasting - Health Effects

[45] http://orthodoxinfo.com/praxis/pr_fasting.aspx

[46] http://orthodoxinfo.com/praxis/pr_fasting.aspx

[47] *Celebration of Discipline The Path to Spiritual Growth* – pg. 51 – by Richard J. Foster– HarperCollins Publishing Inc. – ISBN 0-06-06839-1

[48] *Fasting Can Save Your Life* – Introduction – Dr. Hebert M. Shelton – American Natural Hygiene Society, Inc. – ISBN 0-914532-23-5

[49] *Fasting Can Save Your Life* – Introduction – Dr. Hebert M. Shelton – American Natural Hygiene Society, Inc. – ISBN 0-914532-23-5

[50] *Fasting Can Save Your Life* – pg. 15 – Dr. Hebert M. Shelton – American Natural Hygiene Society, Inc. – ISBN 0-914532-23-5

[51] *Fasting Can Save Your Life* – pg. 19 – Dr. Hebert M. Shelton – American Natural Hygiene Society, Inc. – ISBN 0-914532-23-5

[52] *Fasting Can Save Your Life* – pg. 21 – Dr. Hebert M. Shelton –

American Natural Hygiene Society, Inc. – ISBN 0-914532-23-5

53 *Fasting Can Save Your Life* – pg. 21 – Dr. Hebert M. Shelton – American Natural Hygiene Society, Inc. – ISBN 0-914532-23-5

54 *Fasting Can Save Your Life* – pg. 24 – Dr. Hebert M. Shelton – American Natural Hygiene Society, Inc. – ISBN 0-914532-23-5

55 *Fast Your Way To Health* – pg. 104 - J. Harold Smith – Radio Bible Hour; P.O. Box 99; Newport, TN 37821 – ISBN 0-8407-5776-3

56 *Fasting Can Save Your Life* – pg. 24 – Dr. Hebert M. Shelton – American Natural Hygiene Society, Inc. – ISBN 0-914532-23-5

57 *Fasting Can Save Your Life* – pg. 24 – Dr. Hebert M. Shelton – American Natural Hygiene Society, Inc. – ISBN 0-914532-23-5

58 *The Miracle of Fasting* – by Paul C. Bragg N.D, Ph.D. and Patricia Bragg N.D, Ph.D. – Published in the United States HEALTH SCIENCE; Box 7; Santa Barbara, California 93102 – www.bragg.com - ISBN-13: 978-0-87790-039-9

59 *The Miracle of Fasting* – inside cover page– by Paul C. Bragg N.D, Ph.D. and Patricia Bragg N.D, Ph.D. – Published in the United States HEALTH SCIENCE; Box 7; Santa Barbara, California 93102 – www.bragg.com - ISBN-13: 978-0-87790-039-9

60 *The Miracle of Fasting* – pg. iv – by Paul C. Bragg N.D, Ph.D. and Patricia Bragg N.D, Ph.D. – Published in the United States HEALTH SCIENCE; Box 7; Santa Barbara, California 93102 – www.bragg.com - ISBN-13: 978-0-87790-039-9

61 *The Miracle of Fasting* – pg. iv – by Paul C. Bragg N.D, Ph.D. and Patricia Bragg N.D, Ph.D. – Published in the United States HEALTH SCIENCE; Box 7; Santa Barbara, California 93102 – www.bragg.com - ISBN-13: 978-0-87790-039-9

62 http://naturalhealthperspective.com/tutorials/paul-bragg.html

63 *The Miracle of Fasting* – pg. 53 – by Paul C. Bragg N.D, Ph.D. and Patricia Bragg N.D, Ph.D. –Published in the United States HEALTH SCIENCE; Box 7; Santa Barbara, California 93102 – www.bragg.com - ISBN-13: 978-0-87790-039-9

[64] *The Miracle of Fasting* – pg. 71 – by Paul C. Bragg N.D, Ph.D. and Patricia Bragg N.D, Ph.D. –Published in the United States HEALTH SCIENCE; Box 7; Santa Barbara, California 93102 – www.bragg.com - ISBN-13: 978-0-87790-039-9

[65] *The Miracle of Fasting* – pg. 73 – by Paul C. Bragg N.D, Ph.D. and Patricia Bragg N.D, Ph.D. –Published in the United States HEALTH SCIENCE; Box 7; Santa Barbara, California 93102 www.bragg.com - ISBN-13: 978-0-87790-039-9

[66] *The Miracle of Fasting* – pg. 77 – by Paul C. Bragg N.D, Ph.D. and Patricia Bragg N.D, Ph.D. –Published in the United States HEALTH SCIENCE; Box 7; Santa Barbara, California 93102 – www.bragg.com ISBN-13: 978-0-87790-039-9

[67] *The Miracle of Fasting* – pg. 177 – by Paul C. Bragg N.D, Ph.D. and Patricia Bragg N.D, Ph.D. – Published in the United States HEALTH SCIENCE; Box 7; Santa Barbara, California 93102 www.bragg.com - ISBN-13: 978-0-87790-039-9

[68] *Fasting Can Save Your Life* – pg. 11 – Dr. Hebert M. Shelton – American Natural Hygiene Society, Inc. – ISBN 0-914532-23-5

[69] *Fasting Can Save Your Life* – pg. 13 – Dr. Hebert M. Shelton – American Natural Hygiene Society, Inc. – ISBN 0-914532-23-5

[70] *Fasting Can Save Your Life* – pg. 55 – Dr. Hebert M. Shelton – American Natural Hygiene Society, Inc. – ISBN 0-914532-23-5

[71] *Fasting Can Save Your Life* – pg. 55 – Dr. Hebert M. Shelton – American Natural Hygiene Society, Inc. – ISBN 0-914532-23-5

[72] *Fasting Can Save Your Life* – pg. 57 – Dr. Hebert M. Shelton – American Natural Hygiene Society, Inc. – ISBN 0-914532-23-5

[73] *Fast Your Way To Health* – pg. 107 – J. Harold Smith – Radio Bible Hour; P.O. Box 99; Newport, TN 37821 – ISBN 0-8407-5776-3

[74] *Fast Your Way To Health* – pg. 107 – J. Harold Smith – Radio Bible Hour; P.O. Box 99; Newport, TN 37821 – ISBN 0-8407-5776-3

[75] *Fast Your Way To Health* – pg. 107 – J. Harold Smith – Radio Bible

Hour; P.O. Box 99; Newport, TN 37821– ISBN 0-8407-5776-3

[76] www.roapm.com – About ROA

[77] http://www.wallaceministries.com/Biosketch.html

[78] *Fast Your Way To Health* – pg. 17 – J. Harold Smith – Radio Bible Hour; P.O. Box 99; Newport, TN 37821 – ISBN 0-8407-5776-3

[79] *Fast Your Way To Health* – pg. 55 - J. Harold Smith – Radio Bible Hour; P.O. Box 99; Newport, TN 37821 – ISBN 0-8407-5776-3

[80] *Fast Your Way To Health* – pg. 24 - J. Harold Smith – Radio Bible Hour; P.O. Box 99; Newport, TN 37821 – ISBN 0-8407-5776-3

[81] *God's Chosen Fast* – pg. 118 – by Arthur Wallis – Christian Literature Crusade – ISBN 0-87508-554-7

[82] *How to fast Successfully* – pg. 33 – by Derek Prince – Derek Prince Ministries—International; P.O. Box 19501; Charlotte, NC 28219 – ISBN-13: 978-0-88368-345-3

[83] *C.T. Studd Athlete and Pioneer* – pg. 76 – by Norman P. Grubbs – Zondervan Publishing House; Grand Rapids8, Michigan

Bibliography

American Dictionary of the English Language – Noah Webster 1828 – Published by the Foundation for American Christian Education

Celebration of Discipline The Path to Spiritual Growth – by Richard J. Foster – HarperCollins Publishing Inc. – ISBN 0-06-06839-1

C.T. Studd Athlete and Pioneer – by Norman P. Grubbs Zondervan Publishing House – Grand Rapids Michigan

Experiencing The Depths Of Jesus Christ – by Jeanne Guyon – Seed Sowers Publishing; P.O. Box 3317; Jacksonville, FL 32206 – ISBN-0-940232-00-6

Fasting Can Save Your Life – Dr. Hebert M. Shelton – American Natural Hygiene Society, Inc. – ISBN 0-914532-23-5

Fast Your Way To Health – by J. Harold Smith – Radio Bible Hour; P.O. Box 99; Newport, TN 37821 – ISBN 0-8407-5776-3

God's Chosen Fast – by Arthur Wallis – Christian Literature Crusade – ISBN 0-87508-554-7

Heartbeats of the Holy – by Keith E. Knauss – Printed by Faith Baptist Publications – Ft. Pierce, FL – *www.fbcpublications.com*

How to fast Successfully – by Derek Prince – Derek Prince Ministries – International; P.O. Box 19501; Charlotte, NC 28219 – ISBN-13: 978-0-88368-345-3

King James Bible

Missionary Duplications – 1744 Victoria Ct; Mansfield, OH 44906 – Ldembrador@aol.com

Numbers in the Bible – by Robert D. Johnston – Kregel Publications, as division of Kregel, Inc.; P.O. box 2607; Grand Rapids, MI 49501 – ISBN 0-8254-2965-x

Repentance – Gomez Publications – A ministry of Northwest Bible Baptist Church; 9N889 Nesler Road; Elgin, IL 60123

Shaping History Through Prayer and Fasting – by Derek Prince – Derek Prince Ministries; P.O. Box 19501; Charlotte, NC 28219-9501 – ISBN 978-0-88368-773-4

The Complete Works of Oswald Chambers – Discovery House Publishers – ISBN 1-57293-039-X

The Faith of George W. Bush – by Stephen Mansfield – Charisma House A Strang Company; 600 Rinehart Road; Lake Mary, Florida 32746 – www.charismahouse.com – ISBN 1-59185-242-0

The Man In The Middle – by Timothy S. Goeglein – B&H Publishing Group; Nashville, TN – ISBN 978-4336-7288-0

The Miracle of Fasting – by Paul C. Bragg N.D, Ph.D. and Patricia Bragg N.D, Ph.D. – Published in the United States HEALTH SCIENCE; Box 7; Santa Barbara, California 93102 – www.bragg.com - ISBN-13: 978-0-87790-039-9

The Power of Prayer and Fasting – by Ronnie Floyd –Broadman and Holman Publishers – ISBN O-8054-0164-4

The Spirit World - by Richard W. De Haan – http://www.amazon.com/s/ref=nb_sb_noss?url=search-alias=stripbooks&field-keywords=the+spirit+world+Richard+W.+De+Haan&x=17&y=21

Treasury of David – by Charles Spurgeon

Tribune Democrat – Johnstown, PA – Wednesday, September 11, 2002

World Wide Web